PERSONAL PLACES

Books by Catherine C. Crane

Residential Interiors Today
What Do You Say to a Naked Room?
Personal Places

PERSONAL PLACES

How to Make Your Home Your Own

By Catherine C. Crane

WHITNEY LIBRARY OF DESIGN
an imprint of Watson-Guptill Publications/New York

Copyright © 1982 by Catherine C. Crane

First published 1982 in New York by Whitney Library of Design,
an imprint of Watson-Guptill Publications,
a division of Billboard Publications, Inc.,
1515 Broadway, New York, N.Y. 10036

Library of Congress Cataloging in Publication Data
Crane, Catherine C.
    Personal places.
    1. Interior decoration—Psychological aspects.
2. Buildings—Remodeling for other use. I. Title.
NK2113.C7   747   81-16044
ISBN 0-8230-7422-6   AACR2
ISBN 0-8230-7423-4 (pbk.)

Manufactured in U.S.A.

First Printing, 1982

Edited by Sharon Lee Ryder, Stephen A. Kliment, and Susan Davis
Designed by Jay Anning
Set in 9 point Times Roman

Distributed in Continental Europe by:
  Feffer & Simons, BV
  170 Rijnkade
  Weesp, Netherlands
Distributed throughout the rest of the world except
the United Kingdom by:
  Fleetbooks
  c/o Feffer & Simons, Inc.
  100 Park Avenue
  New York, NY 10017

CONTENTS

ACKNOWLEDGMENTS

First, I'd like to thank Donald J. Carroll, Publisher of *Residential Interiors* magazine, for inventing the idea of doing books based on material published in the magazine, a highly respected journal for professional designers, and, of course, for recommending me to do the books!

I'm grateful to the editors of *Residential Interiors* for their sensitivity and selectivity. The thought-provoking essays and the harmonious interiors presented on the pages of their magazine became my highly refined raw material. I felt like a jeweler creating new designs with previously polished gems. Particular appreciation is due to Susan S. Szenasy and Richard W. Jones, past Editors of the magazine, and Ruth Miller Fitzgibbons, previous Managing Editor. Akiko Busch, Jim Kemp, Lorel McMillan, and Anne Troutman, staff editors, also made important contributions to the magazine and this book.

I'm thankful to Sharon Lee Ryder, my initial Senior Editor at the Whitney Library of Design, for seeing the merits of my psychological approach to this project. It's really a pleasure when such a tuned-in person likes your song and hums along.

I'm grateful to Stephen A. Kliment, my subsequent Senior Editor, for figuring out how to do the Directory.

Akiko Busch did what might be the hardest work of all, processing all the photo permissions. I respect her patience, persistence, and good humor and am indebted to her for her achievement.

Susan Davis, Editor of the Whitney Library of Design, deserves credit for her thoroughness in pinning in all the loose ends that pop up in the process of birthing a book. I also appreciated and *enjoyed* using her as a sounding board.

I want to acknowledge all the magazine contributors whose research and writing form much of the inspiration of this book. They are Jeanne Barnes, Kathleen Beck, Zehra Boccia, Barry Dean, Margaret Drimer, John Duka, Marlene R. Fedin, Richard Horn, Charles Kriebel, Joan Kron, George Nelson, Madeline Rogers, Michael Franklin Ross, AIA, and Sharon Lee Ryder.

Jay Anning, the designer of this book, deserves credit for making you want to look at it and enjoy it.

GETTING-TO-KNOW-YOU QUESTIONNAIRE

It's hard for most of us to know where to begin in the process of making our homes our own. Answering these questions may give you some ideas. Take out a piece of paper and give it a whirl.

Fitting your functions

A convenient home is a comfortable home. What are your requirements?

1. List the people in your household. (Include pets.)

2. List each person's activities. Beside each activity, note the amount of space required and the atmosphere preferred (such as quiet or noisy, private or public, cozy or spacious).

3. Could you accommodate your space requirements in an unconventional home?

4. What furnishings are necessary for each activity?

5. Can any furnishings do double duty?

6. What would make each activity more comfortable or convenient?

7. Who cooks?
   Does this person like to cook alone or with company?
   Does she/he like family/ friends nearby?
   What would make cooking more comfortable and convenient?

8. How do you like to entertain?
   Cozy conversations?
   Large cocktail parties?
   Dinner parties? How big?

Soothing your spirit

With these questions, you're sure to find some idea that will inspire the appropriate ambience for your own home.

9. Where do you live?

10. What inspires you about the past and present of the place where you live?

11. What objects or ideas from the local history appeal to you?

12. Is there a certain sort of architecture that appeals to you?

13. What is it you like about your house?

14. What sort of space makes you feel good?
   Do you like to be cuddled up and cozy?
   Do you require wide open spaces in order to breathe easy?
   Do you sometimes feel one way, sometimes the other?

15. What are your favorite furnishings?
   Things you have:
   Things your mother had:
   Things other people have:

16. Have you inherited furnishings you love?

17. Do you have any sort of collection?
   What is it?
   What charms you most about it?

18. What's your heritage?

19. Where did you spend your past?

20. Is there a certain place in the world where you long to be?

21. What is your favorite vacation spot?

22. Where were you once utterly happy?
   How would you describe this place?

23. What period of history excites you?

24. What period of the past best expresses the feelings you'd like to feel in your home?

25. Who are your heroes? What is it about them that you admire?

26. Where are you and what are you doing when you feel the best?
   How do you imagine you might create that same atmosphere in your home?

27. What comforts you when you're down?

28. What are your interests? Hobbies?

29. What are your happiest fantasies?

30. What's stopping you from creating your favorite mood in your own home?

INTRODUCTION: GETTING PERSONAL

Suffering is out of style. No longer do we have to sublimate ourselves to fit into the rational order imposed upon us by architects or builders. No longer do we have to suffer secret shame for wanting to keep the well-worn or odd-ball objects that our designer wants us to toss out. No longer do we have to feel embarrassed for choosing comfort over "enlightenment." Happily, architects and designers are beginning to see it our way. They have rediscovered "human values." They are up for some softness, sentiment, surprise—some sense of the past.

We, thank God, are getting past the "Modern Movement" that started around the beginning of the century. The Modern Movement, with its emphasis on order, intellectualism, and abstraction, denied essential dimensions of the human experience. Sensuality and spirituality were suppressed. The past was denied, and so, as a matter of fact, was pleasure. Surprise and serendipity were unthinkable—no place for randomness in this rational order. Architects of the Modern Movement saw themselves as social reformers. They thought their buildings would improve people, bring a rational order to human society. They wanted technology to reform culture. Mies van der Rohe, a leader of the Modern Movement, was not ashamed to say: "The individual is losing significance. His destiny no longer interests us."

Well, as they said in the movies, "We're fed up and we're not going to take it any more!" Maybe the mounting years of deprivation have caused enough emotional discomfort to bring awareness. Maybe the human potential movement of the 1970s has had something to do with it, but for whatever reasons, we're at the beginning of an exciting time, a time when the home can be designed to be fulfilling, designed to act as an emotional and spiritual support system.

How can *your* home function as an emotional support system for *you*?

Your home can be designed to save you time, energy, and stress

Do you work at home? Raise children? Cook? Entertain? What are your special needs for doing the things you do comfortably and conveniently? Designing your home accordingly can save you time, effort, and stress. Take cooking, for example. Today Americans seem more interested in cooking and food than ever before, but with more and more women working, fewer and fewer people have the time to make lengthy food preparations. Modern technology provides one solution. Consider the Cuisinart and the microwave oven. Another is to have help in the kitchen. Since few people can afford servants any more, other family members must get into the act of preparing meals, and so too guests. The kitchen can even be designed to inspire assistance. For example, Chinese chef Jim Lee must often clean five pounds of shrimp at a swat. That's a lot of peeling and deveining. To encourage help, he had the shelves under his sink designed to pull out and become a bench where two can sit comfortably together to chat while working.

Designing the kitchen for sociability is efficient. It helps the cook enlist others in meal preparation. If the kitchen is such a pretty place that people want to be there, they'll be around when the celery needs chopping or the soup needs stirring.

The need to save time and energy while preparing healthful, interesting meals has led to a new lifestyle. Cooking and entertaining in the kitchen. Certified Kitchen Designer Florence Perchuck calls it a "celebrity style" (she helped actors Ann Jackson and Eli Wallach create their cozy country kitchen). In addition to increased efficiency, the kitchen today has several positive emotional payoffs. The cook no longer suffers from isolation. She or he is where the action is, having fun. Also the quality of the conversation in the informal kitchen has got to be more refreshing and relaxed than that in the front parlor. You can get a lot of tension off your chest, talking while kneading the bread.

Your bathroom, on the other hand, could be just the place to save your sanity. Do you ever feel that you're on Old MacDonald's Farm? Everybody's mooing and quacking. With everybody *at* you, or telling you their problems (or worse, *your* problems), don't you long for escape? Well, help is at hand. Down the hall, to the right. Yes, that's right. Your bathroom. I'm not suggesting that you lock the door and slit your wrists. Rather, that you run the hot water, pour in the bath salts, strip off your clothes, and soak your troubles away. Relaxing your body is a wonderful way to relax your mind. You could do it with exercise (perhaps with an at-home gym). You could do it with massage, a steam room, a sauna—a bath. Being good to your body will help you not only lengthen, but enjoy your life. Your home, particularly your bathroom, can give you important sensuous support. Some designers feel bathrooms can be almost as refreshing as vacations. They make them into fantasy get-aways. In one couple's home, her bathroom is designed like a Grecian garden, complete with marble tub and classic columns. His simulates a safari. His sunken tub is patterned like tiger's skin.

Today we are more aware than ever before that mental health and physical health are akin. By designing your home to take care of your body, you are doing good things for your head—and health.

Zoning your home for public and private places is also important in relieving stress. Even your kids don't want to be interrupted when they're sharing secrets with friends. And you value your privacy too, don't you?

If you work at home, how can you focus on the business at hand without being distracted by domesticity? How can you relax when your workday is done if you are still in the same physical space? These are problems that designers often confront. The answers are individual. For a dancer, one solution was "building-block" furniture that could be moved out of the way, leaving her loft floor free. For a film producer, it was a projection tower incorporating a dozen projectors. At night, the tower is transformed into a free-floating sculpture. The designer rigged lighting around its edges to create the softer evening illusion.

By addressing your own particular work and leisure needs, a designer can enhance your effectiveness, keeping you from having to climb Everest every day. Why make life harder than it need be? Wouldn't you like to be more effective with less effort?

Your home can be designed to save you money

Interest rates are incredible. Inflation impossible. Fuel costs inhumane. And a lot of other costs insane. (Peanut butter in particular.) How can one get on with gracious living in such an economic mess? Good design can save you money and even sometimes *make* you money.

A Minneapolis stockbroker who uses his home as his office had it designed with symbolism to suggest that he had a way with wealth, that he knew how to make it and spend it. (Encouraging for a client who is nervous about parting with his or her nest egg.) If you work at home, you can design your space to suggest that you do indeed have the qualities that your client or customer may be looking for. It is, as they say, "good business."

In addition your home can be designed to reduce your costs of heating and air conditioning. We're hearing more and more these days about solar houses and other inventive designs that are energy-efficient. Insulation in your attic. Double-glass at your windows, shades, blinds. Roof overhangs that shade too-sunny windows, other areas that suck in the sun in cold weather. Insulating paneled or fabric-covered walls. Wood stoves. Coal stoves. Electric blankets. Down comforters. We are occupied in taking our temperature and in trying to keep it normal.

A lot of us are just shrugging and moving into smaller spaces, less costly to heat and cool. Most of the rest of us are simply forced to live in small spaces because we can't afford the mortgage rates or the rentals on larger ones.

How can you have a sense of wealth and well-being in a small space? Designers can help you create illusions of grandeur—even inexpensively. I'm fond of the fellow with glamorous aspirations who had to move into a dingy one-room flat in Manhattan. He gave himself the illusion of all he wanted by designing his space in the sparkling style of the 30s. He created an Art Deco ambience with shiny and smooth textures and ziggurat shapes. He never darkened the door of an antique shop.

To stretch the seeming sense of space, designers have developed many devices. They link the indoors with the outdoors by enlarging the windows, putting mirrors opposite a view, blurring the difference between indoors and out by continuous colors or plants and flowers. They break down the barriers in the interior by tearing down nonsupportive walls between rooms or covering all walls and floors in the same continuous light neutral color. They choose low, simple, minimal, or multifunctional furniture. They build storage into the architecture. Use vertical designs to make the ceiling seem higher. Mount lighting on the ceiling or walls to make use of all areas of the room and keep clutter off the tables or floor. They arrange furniture on the diagonal to break out of the room's boxy shape. Designers have made it their business to provide a look of luxury in small spaces.

Another point of value. Furnishings used in multipurpose or often-used rooms are worth investing money in. They provide value. The real cost of anything is its initial purchase price, plus its cost of maintenance, divided by its days of usefulness. If something is used heavily or often, it is worth buying better quality. It will last longer and look better. Choose the easy-to-maintain material over the fragile one in these instances. The higher price will be worth the savings in cleaning costs.

As a banker once told me, in times of inflation, it's best to invest in yourself. Investing in yourself can increase your power to produce. An uncomfortable, inconvenient home drains off your energy. A convenient, comfortable, attractive home builds up your energy. It not only makes you look successful, it makes you *feel* successful. And, as we all know, nothing breeds success like success.

Your home can increase your self-esteem and gain you recognition from others

Each of us is special. It is hard to feel so when you walk into another stamped-out apartment or another tract home. Given the spaces that most of us are forced to live in, how can we make our mark? We want to feel cozy and comfortable where we live. We want to belong. On the other hand, we don't want the environment to overwhelm us and eat up our individuality. How can we belong to the group and still celebrate ourselves?

What is it that you especially like about the place where you live? Do you like the scenery outdoors? The romance of the past of the place? By incorporating whatever aspects you like into the design of your own home you can make a connection, relate to the place—gain a sense of belonging. For instance, the designer of a ski lodge out West brought in the grand scale of the outdoors by using rough log furniture. He suggested the past of the place by using Indian drums for coffee tables. A couple in a new house in Nantucket used Chinese porcelains to suggest the romance of the island's past "tea trade." A wealthy international official in a Manhattan skyscraper with a spectacular view used the scintillating city lights as a theme. Mirrors and sparkling lights link his apartment with the excitement outdoors.

Making a connection with the place where you live is a good way to make a connection with the others who live there too. You begin with something in common.

By expressing your own personal interests in your home, you give others the opportunity to appreciate your individuality—and enjoy it. You can express your interests by exhibiting a favorite collection—maybe your bowling trophies, pictures of yachts, old family furniture, or Victorian valentines. You can even use your collection as the inspiration of your whole interior design scheme. Maybe you're enchanted by a certain period of the past, a certain place you've visited. Maybe you have a favorite fantasy. Any of these things could generate the interior design ideas that would make your home a particularly personal place. Conformity is passé today. People are striving to express their individuality so that they may know and appreciate themselves and relate to others in a *real* way.

Not to dare to express yourself is to demean yourself, to rob others of the opportunity to know you and appreciate you. True, we have been conditioned to conformity, but those are machine values, not human ones. During the Modern Movement, Le Corbusier called the home "a machine for living." Seems that we were just interchangeable cogs running around in the machine. We were bound to wear down. Now we no longer equate ourselves with machines nor find ourselves lacking in efficiency and discipline. We've got spirit, soul, eccentricities, and that's what life's all about! By esteeming ourselves and being ourselves we get individual recognition from others. Our homes can support our individuality and express it.

Your home can be designed to give you an exciting new sense of yourself

Did you like Disneyland? Did you like trying on the native clothes, tasting the native foods on your last trip? Do you like James Bond? How did you feel about *Star Wars?* All of these experiences take you out of your ordinary everyday world. They release you from a doing-the-dishes mentality. Fantasy is fun. It adds spice, excitement, surprise to life. Makes you feel more vital. More able to *do* your dreams. Less weighted down with the world.

You can design your home to inspire the same sensations in you. A fellow who moved into an old garage suggested the south of France with white stucco walls, quarry tile floors, and accessories in bright Matisse colors. The woman who never wanted the party to end painted her friends on her bedroom walls, as well as a waiter coming in with champagne. The Hollywood producer who had done everything and was looking for a new experience designed a disco in his home that looks for all the world like an Egyptian tomb. A designer of movie sets made a chair to look like an elephant, a sofa to look like a red cow. As Hamlet said, "There are more things in heaven and earth, Horatio, than are dreamt of in our philosophy."

Dreaming and allowing your dreams to come true in your own home are a wonderful way to create fun and a release from the humdrum. You may just choose some whacky or whimsical accessory, but some sense of surprise provides delicious delight. Like a package all wrapped in ribbon, it's a present to yourself. Don't you deserve it?

You're worth it

Your home can save you time, energy, and stress, make the most of your money, encourage your self-esteem, impress your friends, and inspire a sense of fun. With thoughtful design, your home *can* become your own personal place.

PART ONE:

CLAIMING SPACE

People talk about getting into their own space, but how do you make your home your own? How do you lay claim to the territory? How do you even decide where you want to live?

It's no secret to any of us that real estate costs are high—downright scary. Even if you are endowed with a big beautiful home, the costs of heating it and cooling it these days are enough to raise *your* temperature. Because of the costs of renting, buying, heating, cooling, more and more of us are living in small spaces. Small, stamped-out spaces at that. New buildings are notoriously boring; your warren looks just like the rabbit's next door. Our sensibilities have always been offended by being treated as nobody special. We got used to it and internalized that we probably deserved it. Now there are gurus (and even occasionally architects) who are saying that we deserve to have the space we want. But who can afford it?

First of all, what *is* the space we want? How much space do we need to accommodate the activities we like to indulge in at home? "Colorfield" painter Peter Bradley knew he needed space the size of a barn. Architect Noel Yauch knew he could fit his major living activities into a 20 x 30-foot (6 x 9.2-meter) space in an old Brooklyn brownstone. If you have an idea of the physical space you need to do your thing, you might look for it in unconventional places. Michael Kurt Harris converted an abandoned garage into what he wanted—complete with a special room for his punching bag. A former factory, "knee-deep in oil," became the perfect place for the color-field painter.

What sort of space makes you *feel* good? Some of us love to be cuddled up and cozy. Some of us in the same situation feel like beating down the walls just to get a breath of air. In which category are you? Do you want your home to be a cozy nook or a wide open expanse? Perhaps you would like your home to be designed so you could accommodate both feelings, so you could pick the place to fit your mood. Alan Buchsbaum's client loved expansive space. He found it in an old industrial loft. He also wanted his dining area to be cozy for company. Buchsbaum gave him what he wanted by lowering the ceiling over the dining area to create an air of intimacy.

Is there a certain sort of architecture that appeals to you? Is there a certain place in the world where you long to be? Architect Noel Yauch selected an old home of the Greek Revival style. He loved its classical simplicity. The man in the abandoned garage fantasized about the south of France. He created its ambience with stucco walls, quarry tile floors, and vibrant colors. You can choose your home for its personal attraction to you, or alternately you can use the tools of design to suggest the place where you want to be.

Most of us suffer from ordinary architecture and too little space

What can we do? Most of us are making do. It's not that automatic any more for people to keep trading up for larger homes. The costs are too crazy, and heaven knows, there are many other things eating away at our inflated dollars. And who has attics and basements any more? Where are those wonderful places where we used to stash stuff? Now it's all falling out of our closets when we go in dripping wet to get a bath towel. We have to shove back the frontal attack. We have to find answers to satisfying storage and gracious living in small spaces.

How can we stretch space?

Designers have divined many devices for stretching space. An important and revolutionary (actually pre-Revolutionary) concept is to free rooms from single-purpose. Space can work in many ways. Before 1776, the kitchen was often the family room, office, and entertainment center. Today it may again be. The role of rooms has expanded to suit our actual lifestyle. In my childhood we rarely darkened the door of the dining room. It was reserved for occasions—Thanksgiving, Christmas, or when fancy company was coming. On all other occasions, we ate happily in the kitchen, surrounded by the smells—the aromatic attractions—of the meal prepared. If you ask me what home meant to me, it was that kitchen table. We played poker on it. I did my homework on it. I had coffee and discussed "life" with my mother over it.

Who these days wants to pay off a mortgage on a room rarely used? We are beginning to claim our homes for ourselves, not for the occasional company. Besides, with no servants to wait on us, we don't want to wait on our company like servants. We want to share what we do and where we are with them. Our lifestyle is more informal, homogenized. Other than the romance of our emerging lifestyle, costs have caused us to rediscover the assets of the multipurpose room.

Furniture that we buy for such a room gives us our money's worth. We look at it or use it constantly. It is worth what it costs. A fine piece for a rarely used room doesn't have the same sort of value.

We are making better use of the space we have, but how can we make the space we have look like more?

Link the indoors with the outdoors

One way is to link the smaller interior space with the larger exterior space. This can be done in many ways. Sometimes it's appropriate to enlarge the windows. If plants are on view outdoors, you can bring some indoors to create a connection between indoors and out. It's often a wonderful idea to put a mirror opposite a view. The impact of the view is doubled, and the mirrored wall seems to lose its solidity—its confining control. Of course, if you're blessed with a balcony, you might enclose it and incorporate it into the living area or at least blur the distinction between balcony and living area so that both are seen together as one wonderful space. If, on the other hand, you have the misfortune of a horrible view of a highway or a highrise, you might consider, if possible, a skylight. If all else fails for a connection to the outdoors, go for a walk—to your wallpaper store and check out deep-perspective scenics.

Break down the barriers in the interior

Architects and designers these days are fond of tearing down the non-supportive walls between rooms to create the sense of a larger interior space. Then they link all areas by covering the walls and the floor in the same continuous light neutral color. Barriers between areas disappear, and the entire space seems open and airy.

How do the designers define different functional areas without walls? By furniture arrangement, by area rugs, by floor levels, by ceiling heights, by see-over or see-through partitions. The idea is to provide a sense of place without destroying the sense of space.

Architect Noel Yauch tore down the walls between the parlors of his Greek Revival house to make one great big living space for himself and his family. The backs of chairs define the living and the dining areas. A 4-foot (1.2-meter) Formica partition hides the cooking from the dining area, while allowing the cook to converse with her customers. For his client, architect Alan Buchsbaum replaced a dividing wall with pivoting storage cabinets. With the cabinets in the open position, the two rooms seem like one open expanse. With the cabinets closed, the rooms seem separate and cozy.

To conquer cramped quarters in a Florida condominium, designers Edward Garcia and Eleanor Taubmen removed the corner walls of a room adjacent to the living room. As a result the two rooms flow together, and each room seems less confined. To retain a sense of separation, however, the designers raised the floor of the second room. Designer Sandra Nunnerley raised the floor in the center of her living space to give a sense of sunken privacy to her office at the room's end. In the high-ceilinged, narrow corridor of a typical tenement, architects Muller and Murphy suspended a diagonal block from the ceiling to make the place somewhere special.

Continuity of color stretches space

A continuous color on walls and floors is the most effective way to unify and simplify space. A pale color reflects light, so it makes a place seem more airy and open. A pale neutral color is, in addition, restful and easy to live with.

When the large furniture matches the walls or floor, it seems to disappear into the background and take less space. This is a favorite designer device for tricking the eye and creating the illusion of openness. The same goes for matching the windows to the walls. The same color will unify the windows with the walls to simplify and smooth out the space.

With continuous pale, neutral color on the walls, floor, and large furniture, designers often use a variety of texture to create interest in the room. For example, the walls may be softly upholstered, the floors may be hard, slick tile, and there may be something rough or nubby in upholstery or accessories.

In a scheme like this, contrast in color often comes in accessories. This contrast can set off important accessories or even enhance those that aren't so exceptional. An added advantage of this scheme is that you can change the entire mood of the room simply by changing the accessories. There's flexibility in simplicity.

Furniture is low, simple, minimal

The less confusion that meets the eye, the more open and unconfining the room. Low furniture makes the ceiling seem higher, and simple modular seating is a favorite for designers of small spaces. You can get a lot of seating space without a lot of shapes and forms.

The less furniture there is, the more space there is. Designers wrack their brains to find the simplest possible solution to their clients' many requirements. Sandra Nunnerley, for example, built a bookcase into the end of her custom-created sofa. Multifunctional furniture, such as this, is an important answer to beautifying and simplifying small spaces.

Platforms are popular. They can be used as a sleeping surface, a sitting surface, a table, or even a backrest for someone sitting on the floor. Glass and acrylic are favorite materials for tables because they take no visual space. Furniture surfaced in metal or mirror not only visually disappears, it creates space by reflection. However, most furniture tends to be either so massive that it looks like a structural part of the architecture or so light in scale that it doesn't intrude into the space.

Wherever possible, storage is built into the architecture

If you need a lot of storage space, you might build storage closets along one wall and then cover them all in mirror. Then you'll gain space in two ways—you'll supply storage while creating the illusion of openness.

Bookcases built up the walls pluck storage space out of the air. Flip-down surfaces can create tabletops for a desk or a bar. Cabinets built against the walls might have tops used for display or buffet or for desk or seating surfaces.

Diagonals make the room seem larger

A diagonal is the longest line you can draw through a rectangular or square space. A diagonal line also has energy; it seems to push the walls away, making them appear farther away. Designers Barbara Schwartz and Barbara Ross of Dexter Design used the diagonal to make a multipurpose place of a boy's room. In a typical tenement a diagonal platform in one corner breaks up the boxiness of the room. In a dining room/office a wallpaper of a diagonal design gives energy and excitement to the space. In another apartment diagonal divisions create illusions of extra rooms.

Verticals make the ceiling seem higher

Tall trees, vertical blinds, floor-to-ceiling uprights (perhaps holding storage shelves)—all these vertical lines draw the eye up and down. The eye, in its journey, has the illusion of going a greater distance than it is. Suddenly, the ceiling seems higher. Like Mandrake the magician, you too can become the master of illusion.

Allover, even lighting can make a room seem larger

Track lighting that washes the walls and doesn't clutter up the table tops with lamps is a good solution to a small space. Wall-mounted fixtures work well too. Mirror and metal are two materials often used in small rooms because they reflect the light even into dark corners and help waste no space in shadows. For an especially dramatic effect, you might illuminate the underside of a raised platform with fluorescent tube lighting. It creates a floating feeling. What could be more open and airy than providing a sense of weightlessness?

In this chapter you will see how designers defy real dimensions and create the illusion of openness. Their different methods give individuality to interiors that started as rather inefficient or inhumane spaces.

OUTFITTING A 19TH-CENTURY BROWNSTONE FOR 20TH-CENTURY LIVING

Architect Noel Yauch saw the potential in the place. He thought the space would be adequate for his needs, and he liked the architecture. The modest Brooklyn brownstone had been built around 1840 in the Greek Revival style, a style notable for its simplicity and symmetry. The first floor living space was divided into front and back parlors connected with a long narrow foyer. Each room had a fireplace centered on the outside wall and a large window on the end wall. How did Yauch adapt this place to his own living style?

He tore down the walls

Small separate rooms may have worked well in the 19th century when life was more formal and the family preferred some separation from the servants. Now, when we tend to wait on ourselves and rush around at a faster pace, we like more openness and informality. Architect Yauch, experienced in architectural renovation, tore down the walls to create a pleasing 20 x 30-foot (6 x 9-meter) open space. Yauch allowed the two fireplaces to define the furniture groupings. It was natural to put a sofa opposite a fireplace and gather a couple of chairs on either side. The second fireplace was an obvious focus for the dining grouping.

He gave the place the sense of an entrance

It's often disconcerting to walk into a place and be faced with the back of a sofa. It doesn't seem so welcoming. To overcome this feeling, Yauch suggested a gracious grand entrance. Opposite the fireplace wall and centered between the fireplaces, the architect erected two supporting columns to suggest a doorway. The columns' simple lines and symmetrical placement are altogether appropriate to the original architecture. With a centered doorway, the sofa simply seems to define the traffic path.

A 4-foot partition separates the kitchen from the dining room

Since symmetry and balance were themes taken from the original architecture, it was natural to build some structure to balance the sofa on the other end of the room. It was also natural to want to hide the kitchen from the diners on the other side. A 4-foot (1.2-meter) Formica partition hides a butcher block counter and workspace on one side, but still allows the cook to converse with others in the room.

Yauch used many devices to emphasize openness

Continuity of color is a big one. The glazed quarry tile floor and the walls are white. White Formica is the material of the sofa frame, the kitchen partition, and the storage cabinets along the fireplace wall. These large white entities fade into the architecture to stretch the space. Chairs in the conversational area are white canvas, further emphasizing the clean simplicity of the scheme.

Since the ceiling was a rather low 9½ feet (2.9 meters), architect Yauch gave the illusion of greater height and openness by keeping the furniture low. For example, the cabinets along the fireplace wall are only 23 inches (58.4 centimeters) high. The rebuilt stairs sport a low 16-inch (40.6-centimeter) balustrade with a plywood rail. Making use of every inch, Yauch fit storage cabinets flush under the stairs.

To open the interior to the outdoors, the windows on the end walls were emphasized or enlarged. The front bay window was refitted; the rear window opposite was enlarged. Plants at both windows visually connect the indoors with the outdoors.

Photography by Elliot Fine

Adaptability and easy maintenance are incorporated

Various lighting sources allow the manipulation of mood. Recessed lighting provides illumination for work surfaces in the kitchen, general illumination elsewhere. Track lights focus on wall art works. Unobtrusive standing lamps by the sofa provide an intimate light for reading.

The top of the Formica storage cabinets along the fireplace wall can be used as a buffet for entertaining or as display space for objects of seasonal or personal preference. Formica and quarry tile materials are easy to clean. The allover design of this living space is so simple that too much time needn't be taken up in dusting detail. The design provides a basic background for relaxed living.

The symmetry and simplicity of the original structure have been respected in this adept adaptation to 20th-century living.

Sources

Lighting: LIGHTOLIER track lighting; HARRY GITLIN recessed lighting. Couch: WORKBENCH. Farmer chairs: STENDIG. Surfaces in kitchen: FORMICA and butcher block. Stove: CROWN. Tile: glaze quarry tile by LONDONDERRY, OHIO at ELON TILE in New York.

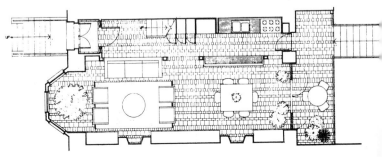

CONVERTING AN ABANDONED
GARAGE INTO A HOME

How can you express yourself on a low budget? If you know your needs, you might find an unconventional, inexpensive way to accommodate them.

Michael Kurt Harris of The Design Corps eschewed expensive real estate. He converted an abandoned garage into his home. Along with his partner/sister Lesley, he saw that the small 15 x 22-foot (4.6 x 6.7-meter) building in West Hollywood could be adapted to his needs. The garage had been divided into two units during World War II—a storage space and a small work area, each with its own bathroom.

Restructuring provided the comforts of home

The design team knocked out the dividing wall between the two spaces, created one bathroom, and added a kitchen. The largest area is used for living/sleeping. The smaller open area is used for working out. It features an enormous 75-pound (34-kilogram) punching bag suspended from the ceiling. Why not? It's what Harris likes to do. To open up and air out the space, two skylights and several windows were added.

Clever design devices sustain a happy fantasy

One window of the abandoned garage faced a view of a new highrise and a freeway, symbols of real life in West Hollywood. To get away from the frenetic sense of urban activity, to create a psychic separation and an air of peace and privacy, the design team blocked this window. Instead, they emphasized the view of the lemon tree in the newly pruned garden. Mike Harris says he feels "like I'm in the south of France." The colors and textures of his home sustain the illusion. Walls are white stucco, and the floor in the living area is quarry tile. Colors have the vibrancy and vitality of those washed in the Mediterranean sunshine.

Colors are not chosen for their conventional symbolism, but for their emotional impact

According to Lesley Harris, "Most men feel they have to live with dark colors, like rusts and greens, in a warm and woodsy atmosphere. We wanted to prove that it is possible for a man to live in a space that is not furnished in such dark colors."

Not only do the bright colors suggest the Mediterranean sunshine, they have more direct emotional impact. Lesley and Michael Harris understand the healing and therapeutic effects of color. Mike Harris explains: "Greens and golden yellows are healing colors—one calms or relaxes the nerves while the other works in a more active or stimulating way. Highly spiritual purples are meditative and can induce sleep." Particleboard blocks, painted bright green and purple, give interest and impact to Harris's living area. A golden yellow coatrack further sparks the space.

Bright colors have a practical purpose too

Bright colors have such a strong effect that they are a wonderful substitute for expensive artifacts and accessories. They can make a simple space interesting and exciting. They can also lighten and brighten areas that would otherwise be dark and dreary.

Leslie and Michael Kurt Harris of The Design Corps solved practical and emotional needs in a totally simple, if unconventional, way. They addressed the essential issues with imagination.

Photography by Robert Stein

Sources

The particleboard blocks, painted green and purple, are custom made. The mattress and pillow coverings, also custom, are from parachute pack cloth made by UNITEX. Coatrack: VELCA/LUCCI & ORLANDINI. Ceramic vase: PICASSO. Lamp: JANUS ET CIE. Mugs and thermos: HELLER DESIGNS INC. Bertoia chair: KNOLL INTERNATIONAL. Punching bag: TUF-WEAR.

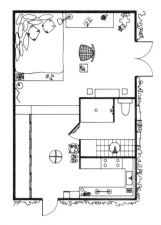

TRANSFORMING A FORMER FACTORY

"Color-field" painter Peter Bradley needed space—lots of it. He needed a big area in which to work, to spread out his paints and canvases. He also needed a place to live. His budget, however, was not up to the prices of conventional residential and commercial real estate.

A former factory in lower Manhattan, "knee-deep in oil," made his eyes light up. Grubby as it was, the price was right, and the acreage ample.

How to make it habitable? Bradley got in touch with British-born architect Paul Heyer, author of the book *Architects on Architecture*. He, if anybody, would know how to transform this space. Given a total budget of only $10,000, Heyer accepted a real challenge.

Heyer made Bradley's hobby into the focal point of the space

What do you do with a vast empty space to make it comforting and personal? Heyer was inspired by Bradley's hobby. Bradley loves to cultivate rare orchids in his spare time. Architect Heyer knew how to double the pleasure, double the fun (without chewing gum). He created a multisided greenhouse, not only to accommodate Bradley's hobby, but as a device to define the space. He designed the shape of the greenhouse so that it would have two sides exposed to what would be the living area, one side backed to the bathtub, one side enlightening a windowless interior study, and yet another side angled to the entry to provide an alluring invitation into the interior. In the living area, the greenhouse provides a focal point for the conversational grouping. One of its glass sides is intentionally angled to reflect the outside. At night one can revel in a double view of sparkling city lights. And imagine the sybaritic luxury of soaking in the tub while gazing at exotic orchids in a lush landscape of gorgeous greens. One idea provides so many solutions.

Pipes and plumbing needed to be accommodated

The artificially lit, climatically controlled, glassed greenhouse needed water, and so did a bathroom, a kitchen, and a studio sink. How to accommodate plumbing pipes with the least architectural alteration? Heyer arranged the bathroom, greenhouse, kitchen, and sink along a diagonal line for the utmost efficiency. To conceal the plumbing pipes along the floor in the area between the greenhouse and the kitchen, he raised a carpeted platform.

A lowered ceiling and a raised floor give variety to the space

The former factory had a long narrow entry. To give interest and intimacy to this area, Heyer installed a bookshelf wall and lowered the ceiling. One passes through the cozy enclosure of the entry onto the raised platform and then into the openness of the living area. Here, Heyer has articulated three different experiences of space. He has suppressed the sameness of the former factory and provided pleasure.

Furnishings are underplayed to emphasize the art

Furnishings are simple, spare, classic. The conversational grouping floats in the center of the space to leave the walls free for art. Furnishing colors are neutral. These neutral tones serve to set off the excitement of the art. This is, after all, an artist's home.

Sources

Chairs, coffee table: KNOLL INTERNATIONAL. Sofas: Custom.

(1) Painting studio, (2) entry, (3) kitchen, (4) study, (5) bath, (6) living/dining, (7) bedroom.

BUILDING A LOFT WITHIN A LOFT

Where in Manhattan but in an abandoned industrial building in the SoHo district could one find such spatial grandeur at a relatively practical price? Having landed the loft as his own, the client wanted to make it his home, but to do nothing to diminish its exhilarating openness. Alan Buchsbaum, partner in Design Coalition, took on the job of converting the former cord factory into a livable loft.

A sense of soaring space

How did Buchsbaum define different areas of activity without confining the sense of space? He built no vertical walls to obstruct the view throughout. Instead, he constructed a loft between two pillars through a central section of the space. Functionally, the loft provides a sleeping, dressing, and desk area on the upper level. Below, the lowered ceiling contributes a sense of coziness to the kitchen and dining area. On either side of the loft, there is a sense of soaring space. Ironically, lowering the ceiling in one area emphasizes its height in others.

There is further refinement. Note that the bed seems to be raised on a platform. Note also that the ceiling in the dining area is 18 inches (45.7 centimeters) higher than that of the kitchen. By this simple change in floor/ceiling height, Buchsbaum has given further definition to two functional areas.

The walls of the loft are only 24 inches (61 centimeters) in

Photography by Norman McGrath

width, keeping their look light. The loft wall is narrow enough to balance the width of the pillars it crosses. Buchsbaum has achieved a harmonious blending of the new and the old.

Spare furnishings double the impact of the space

Like the loft, furnishings are second hand, but nonetheless dramatic. When surrounded by space, pieces seem sculptural. In a corner of its own, the piano has particular panache. It works the other way too. To emphasize the grandeur of the space, the furnishings are few. "By keeping the room completely open, the space maintains itself," notes Buchsbaum.

Sources

Matte glaze ceramic tile on floor: MID-STATE TILE. Felt sculpture on left wall of living room by ROBERT MORRIS. Breuer chairs: THONET. Sofa: KNOLL INTERNATIONAL. Kitchen cabinets: LEWIS LES-CARE KITCHENS. Kitchen cabinets surfaced in tile by MID-STATE.

ACCOMMODATING COLLECTIONS IN A SMALL SPACE

Waitman Martin owns a showroom to the trade in Dallas. Some objects he can't bear to sell, so he buys them himself and brings them home. One might expect his smallish Dallas co op to be utter clutter, but it's not. It's a credit to his designers, Bill Farrington, ASID, and Don Reid, ASID.

The designers stretched the space

To extend the interior space, the designers enclosed parts of an existing balcony. To overcome the visual obstruction of an interior column, they clad it in mirror. They placed low mirrored cabinets on either side of the column to divide the room into two

functional areas without confining the sense of space. These cabinets also provide a convenient pedestal for art, which is reflected in the column and enjoyed from both areas.

Mirror in the dining room provided an answer for storage and space stretching. Floor-to-ceiling storage cabinets covered in mirror conceal storage and give

an open aspect to the enclosed space. The dining table is see-through glass on an acrylic base.

Coherence of color unifies and simplifies the space

When you want to emphasize accessories, it's best to underplay the background walls and floor. Walls and floor here are a neu-

Photography by Louis Reens

tral camel color. They are distinguished by a difference in texture. The floors are hard and shiny, while the walls are soft and upholstered. For even more emphasis on accessories, you can underplay the large furniture and the window coverings. Here, the large furnishings and window coverings blend into the background. The floor-to-ceiling windows are covered with camel-colored, slim-slat horizontal blinds. The large modular seating system in the living room (inset, bottom) is upholstered in

the same camel velvet that covers the walls. In the small conversation area (left), the roll-arm sofa is upholstered in an understated pattern that blends the color of the walls with white.

Accessories and art objects are emphasized

With everything else underplayed, the eye is drawn to the objects of importance. An eight-panel Chinese screen in cream and green is the focal point of the small conversation area. In the

living room, it's an antique Chinese rug. In the dining room, it's a collection of precious porcelains. For added warmth, each arrangement is accented with orange.

Sources

Camel-color velvet: LONDON HOUSE. Blinds: LEVOLOR.
Small conversational area (left): Roll-arm sofa: MARTIN/BRATTRUD. Sofa upholstery: S. HARRIS. Bergère and oval-backed chairs: MGM. Bergère upholstery: CLAR-

ENCE HOUSE. Bronze sculpture on mirrored cabinets: "Embrace" by VICTOR SALMES. Large-scale Chin Lun palace jardiniere: LOS ANGELES COUNTY MUSEUM.
Dining room (right): Glass and acrylic table, custom made by PAUL JONES. Dining chairs: MGM. Dining chair upholstery: PAYNE & CO.
Living room (inset, bottom): Modular seating group: VLADIMIR KAGAN. Coffee table: PAUL JONES.

EXPANDING A CRAMPED CONDO

I t sounds glorious to move to Florida. The weather is wonderful, and you have the openness of all outdoors. But what about the interior space? The price might be higher than you want, and the space less than you're used to. Still you want to feel wide open and wonderful. How can you avoid feeling cramped in a small space?

Space stretching was the problem faced by the Northern widower who wanted to make his permanent home in one of Miami's newest international condominium resort complexes, Turnberry Isle Yacht and Racquet Club. The two-bedroom, two-bath condominium he acquired totalled a modest 1,600 square feet [150 square meters] (including the terrace). He wanted a free feeling and a place to sleep his grown children when they came to visit.

Enter designer Edward Garcia and his associate, Eleanor Taubmen of Design International, Inc.

To stretch space, the designers blurred the distinction between indoors and out

The terrace wraps around part of the living area. To filter the strong southern light, but to keep the space-stretching connection between indoors and out, the designers chose see-through sliding raffia panels for the floor-to-ceiling windows (see picture, bottom right). To bring this air of openness indoors, the designers chose materials for the interior that would reflect the light and the view. The back of the kitchen wall faced at an angle into the living area. The designers mirrored this wall to reflect the view (see picture, bottom right). To create a parallel to the kitchen wall, they filled in the corner opposite with a triangular stainless steel and copper wall unit. Made of reflective materials, the wall unit passes on the lilting lightness of the sunshine (see picture, top left). It also provides a focus for a simple seating grouping oriented in the direction of the

view. (A ledge at the bottom of the unit can be used for additional seating.)

The designers removed the corner walls of the second bedroom

With the action in the living area designed in the diagonal direction, the corner walls of the second bedroom seemed more than ever to intrude into the living space. The designers removed those walls to keep the space flowing freely. To distinguish this space from the living area, they raised the floor by building a carpeted platform. To give the floor an open, floating feeling they illuminated it from underneath. The room was made to function as a den, an extension of the living area, but it also works well as a second bedroom when children or other company come. The L-shaped sofa built into the corner incorporates a sofa bed. There is a convenient closet opposite the window wall, and next to the closet (under colorful acrylic sculptures) there is a custom storage unit containing a television and stereo equipment. What could be cozier than watching TV from bed?

The dining area and bar fit logically on either end of the kitchen

It was natural to place the dining area on the end of the kitchen nearest the terrace. The bar was placed in an internal space between the entry and the other end of the kitchen. (You can see the bar in the foreground of the picture above, left.) The back of the bar was glamorized with mirror. A custom stainless steel and glass cabinet for storage also multiplies the light in this internal space. A dropped ceiling over the bar emphasizes the area and echoes the raised floor of the den diagonally opposite. A white floor-to-ceiling grille distinguishes the entry from the bar. Its open structure, of course, does nothing to confine the sense of space.

Photography by Dan Forer

The continuous color beige unifies all areas and opens them to each other

The walls, the floors, the ceilings, the furniture—all are beige. With no variety of color in these major areas, subtle interest is achieved by variations in texture. There is a hard tile floor in the living area and a soft carpeted floor in the den; a nubby weave on the chairs by the bar and a smooth pigskin suede on the chairs in the living area. Add to that the textured interest of burlap on the walls.

Bright color accents perk up the place

A brightly patterned Dhurrie rug defines the conversation area in the living room. Its colors are picked up in pillows, apples, art, and other accessories.

The designers of this Miami condominium have defied real dimensions and created the illusion of openness.

Sources

Stainless steel and copper wall unit: DESIGN INTERNATIONAL by OSCAR CABINET. Living room chairs: SAPORITI ITALIA through CASA BELLA. Bar chairs: RIMA through M.W.G. Accessories: PENGELLY COLLECTIONS. Sculpture: ZUNIGA through GALERIE 99.

Living room area rug: EDWARD FIELDS. Flooring: ENDURANCE FLOOR. Dining chairs: BRICKEL ASSOC. Window panels: WEAVER'S DOMAIN. Sofa: STENDIG. Coffee table: JOHN MASCHERONI. Den: Wallcoverings: S.M. HEXTER. Wall lights: BOYD LIGHTING. Carpeting: SAVNIK & CO. Side table: KNOLL INTERNATIONAL. Coffee table: CUSTOM BY IBERIA. Upholstery fabric: BRUNSCHWIG & FILS. L-shaped sofa: LOUIS MITTMAN. Painting: LARRY ZOX. Acrylic sculptures: VASA.

A DIAGONAL IS THE LONGEST LINE

Designing in the diagonal dimension is a way to stretch space. A diagonal is the longest line you can draw through a rectangular or square space, and it almost seems to push the walls away.

In a teenage boy's bedroom, a carpeted platform positioned on the diagonal simplifies the traffic flow. One can go directly from the entrance to the door at the rear of the room. Because the platform creates one continuous long line, the distance from wall to wall seems greater than before.

The diagonal platform unifies and simplifies a lot of activities

As we've seen before, unifying and simplifying a space makes it seem larger. Confusion and contrast make spaces seem smaller. With their diagonal design, Barbara Schwartz, ASID, and Barbara Ross of Dexter Design, Inc., provided places for sleeping, reading, watching TV, storing stereo equipment and records, and growing plants.

Parallel repetition of the diagonal line creates harmony

To balance the room and create a sense of harmony, the designers wanted to repeat the diagonal line on the other side of the room. To do so, they tore down two walls of a boxy closet by the entrance and instead built shelves diagonally across the remaining two walls. They designed a custom-made desk with sides slanted on the diagonal and repeated the shape in shelves.

A monochromatic color scheme serves to simplify

Walls, window, desk, shelves are all cream colored. The platform is covered in a dark brown matched to the existing carpet. Furnishings seen against the floor are also dark brown. Covered in tan, the mattress makes a transition from the pale walls to the dark floors. Only accessories—flowers, pillows, and plants—deviate from the monochromatic, neutral scheme.

The simple scheme is adaptable to different ages and stages

The teenage boy for whom the space was designed absolutely did not want the usual trite "boy's bedroom." His parents wanted a design that could convert to their own use when their son went off to college and readapt when he came home on vacations. Schwartz and Ross integrated everybody's interests in their simple solution.

Sources

Project Director: BOB COLE. General Contractor: WASCON-BURNS. Custom desk, shelving, box-stand for TV, all surfaced in FORMICA. Round lamps on wall: LIGHTING ASSOCIATES. Window blinds: LEVOLOR. Small tables and chair: CASTELLI FURNITURE. Plants: PLANT SPECIALISTS. Carpet on platform: ESQUIRE CARPET. Quilted fabric bedspread: THORP. Fabric on pillows: ABRAHAM-ZUMSTEG. Sculpture from ALEXANDER F. MILLIKEN GALLERY.

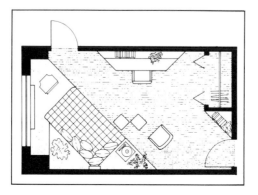

DIAGONAL DIVISIONS CREATE THE ILLUSION
OF ADDITIONAL ROOMS

Wayne Berg is a realistic architect. Although he is in the business of shaping space, he knows that clients in rental apartments don't want to get involved in expensive architectural renovations. They want to take their investments with them when they move. Berg also knows that most of us suffer from the allover ordinariness of urban rental apartments. Their predictability is downright dreary. We want excitement, surprise—not to mention more room.

In the Eftakhari apartment pictured here, Berg has created the illusion of two additional rooms. In the bedroom he placed a storage system at a 45°-angle to the long wall. The storage system not only breaks up the rectangularity of the room, provides storage space and an interesting backdrop for the bed, it defines a little dressing room behind—conveniently adjacent to the bath.

In the living room as well, a diagonal division creates the illusion of an additional room. You know how awkward it is to walk in an entrance and find yourself instantly obvious to everyone in the living room? Berg has created a transition space. By drawing a diagonal from the long wall of the living room toward the door, he has created a sense of separation. The diagonal is an open-work wall that does not confine the living space; instead it provides display space for plants or other objects. The triangulated shape behind the open wall becomes a delicious stolen space for a separate study—complete with the convenient features of a large desk top and a wall full of books. Giving additional impact to the sense of separation, the wooden floor in this area contrasts with the carpet elsewhere.

To complete the triangle and give grandeur to the entrance, Berg has placed two columns to the left of the front door. These columns (actually cardboard tubes) provoke bemused allusion to the architectural refinements of buildings of the past.

Photography by Norman McGrath

Sources

Bed and peach spread: FRANK A. HALL. Custom cabinetry: PERRY DEANGELIS.

DIAGONALS SCULPT SPACE IN A TYPICAL TENEMENT

The ceilings were too high, the corridor too narrow, and the rooms too boxy. This typical tenement was not a space suitable to the spirit of artist Alan Schlussel. A painter and a teacher, Schlussel longed for a relaxed retreat from the frenzy of life in Manhattan. His spirit sought soothing and stretching, not confinement in a predictable stamped-out space.

Architects Louis Muller and William Murphy broke through the psychological confinement of the ordinary without actually breaking down walls or making significant structural changes.

A mirror on the wall perpendicular to the window creates openness

Mirrors allow the imagination to overcome the confinement of concrete walls. A partition built out from the wall gives architectural definition to the placement of the mirror. It advances; the mirror recedes. This in-out play breaks down the boring sameness of the wall. It evokes interest, intrigue, illusion.

A diagonal platform breaks up the boxiness of the room

A diagonal platform under the mirror further dissolves the corner of the room. It is as if the confining square box had a corner torn off, providing the opportunity for escape. As we all know, escape becomes less important if we know it is possible.

A diagonal block suspended from the ceiling stretches the corridor

A huge diagonal block is wedged into place over the entry and suspended to give the illusion of being disconnected. Again the architects have intrigued us.

Sources

Sofa and armchair: B & B AMERICA. Glass coffee table: ARCHITECTURAL SUPPLEMENTS. Painting: ALAN SCHLUSSEL. Red Corbusier chair: ATELIER INTERNATIONAL. Standing lamp: CASTELLI FURNITURE. Dining room lighting: HARRY GITLIN. Green "Selene" stacking chairs: CASTELLI FURNITURE. Dining table top: Custom "filled" travertine.

Photography by Elliot Fine

STORAGE SOLUTIONS BUILT OUT FROM THE ARCHITECTURE

them and thus seem to become background—part of the architecture. The horizontal shelves are black. This contrast draws attention and sets off the accessories on the shelves. Both the desk and the bar feature dropdown work surfaces, creating additional space when wanted.

Repetition of colors makes the place seem like one big space

"I really wanted it to look like one big space," admits Lipton. "But since it isn't I repeated the same patterns and colors." Lipton chose furnishings for color coordination—and for flexibility.

Notice how she deployed a department store sectional. Two armless units are arranged at a right angle to the wall-long banquette. Three units are joined forming a sofa facing the banquette and the art objects above. The den is furnished with one armless sectional and an ottoman. These neutral taupe units spread throughout the living area create a sense of unity and an appealing sense of softness.

The dining table ("It's actually sold as a desk") is of a wood tone that complements the floor, the built-in banquette, and a wood-frame chair in the conversational circle. Again, there's an even distribution of color.

Small objects on the wall create a sense of space around them

"You can create space with tensions between sizes and forms," Lipton explains. "They're all connected. If I need more space, I'll hang something very small—like an icon—on the wall and I will have made that much more space. Hanging a collection, in fact, is fascinating." Indeed, in this interior the small sculptures and low-hung pictures do seem to emphasize the expanse of the white wall around them.

Sources

Dining table: ZOGRAPHOS (fabric: ABRAHAM ZUMSTEG). Chairs: VANLEIGH FURNITURE (fabric: BRICKEL ASSOCIATES). Lacquer table: INTREX (accessories: BLOOMINGDALE'S). Tableware: MACY'S, B. ALTMAN, BLOOMINGDALE'S, ANGELA ZITO. Sculpture: KARL MANN ASSOCIATES. Throw pillows: ANGELA ZITO (fabric: ABRAHAM ZUMSTEG, CLARENCE HOUSE, INTERNATIONAL FELT). Sectional seating: B. ALTMAN. Scissor chair: BRICKEL ASSOCIATES (Ward Bennett). Coffee table: KNOLL INTERNATIONAL. Ottomans: ATELIER INTERNATIONAL (fabric: JACK LENOR LARSEN). Rug: BESHAR. Shades: HOLLAND SHADES. Wall hanging, planter, occasional table: KARL MANN ASSOCIATES. Wall sculpture: HARMER ROOKE GALLERY. Lamps: KOCH & LOWY, INC., LIGHT INC. Bar: INTREX. Accessories: MITSU, AZUMA, HENRI BENDEL, BLOOMINGDALE'S.

Who ever has enough storage space? What apartment dweller hasn't faced sentiment as sediment? Saving stuff from your past can crowd your living space in the present. What to do? Dudley Brauner was smart in trusting designer Elizabeth Lipton to come up with a solution. That New York designer believes in built-ins built out from the architecture.

A banquette matches the floor; vertical storage matches the walls

Lipton built a storage banquette matching the wood of the floor. "This is what I mean by building around the architectural elements," Lipton explains. "If you use the same material for the built-ins as you do for the floor, they really are part of the floor." Extending from the living room window right to the den, the unit functions like a giant, elongated toy chest. Flush tops on piano hinges lift up easily to reveal a wealth of storage space below. The height and depth of the unit were carefully chosen for flexibility. The unit functions as a table for the adjacent chairs, as a display surface, and even more importantly, as additional seating in the conversational circle.

For further functionality Lipton converted the dining area to a den. To create a desk and a bar without cluttering the small space with furniture, she built vertical units on either side of the kitchen door. The supportive uprights match the wall behind

Photography by Frank Kolleogy

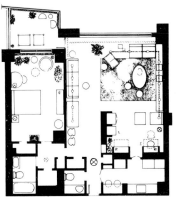

YOU-CAN-TAKE-IT-WITH-YOU-WHEN-YOU-GO STORAGE

No matter what the price, most urban highrise apartments are boring boxes. Interior architectural interest seems to be an asset of another era. However, most of us long for design distinction as well as the contemporary conveniences of dishwashers and such.

People in rental spaces often don't want to solve the problem by built-ins or architectural alteration. They don't want to pad the pockets of their landlords by abandoning these architectural assets when they move. For a client with a bunch of books, designer Thomas Boccia invented an ingenious answer.

Floor-to-ceiling columns of shelves provide storage and architectural interest

To accommodate the client's vast collection of books, as well as her stereo and TV, Boccia built ten columns of varying widths. All of ceiling height, the vertical columns pull storage space from the air while seeming to stretch the height of the standard room.

Designed to be movable, the columns can be changed and rearranged as the client desires. They can be grouped in clusters or lined up against a wall like a conventional bookcase. They can be taken to the truck on moving day. Arranged strategically around the room as pictured, the columns act as space dividers, articulating areas and defining the traffic flow. Banded on the bottom with carpeting matching the floor, the columns seem architecturally anchored. (The band of carpeting has practical aspects too. It prevents scuff marks while cleaning or moving the columns.)

Boccia has used color and lighting to give the columns additional architectural excitement. He painted the columns in a variety of soft sherbet colors. The sense of softness unifies the columns and mollifies their hard, straight lines. The distinctive difference in the hues gives each column individuality, solitary stature. The harmony unifies the space; the variety excites it.

Ordinary picture-frame lamps are mounted on each column. Not only have they the practical purpose of illuminating the book titles, but seen from behind, they set the column aglow by illuminating the space around it. The columns gain additional excitement and architectural impact.

Although clearly modern in mood, these columns allude to the architecture of the past. One is reminded of ancient temples, where the structure is supported by columns. Boccia's contemporary columns succeed in giving the illusion of architecture while, in fact, they give actual support to his client's individual needs.

Tables in the conversational grouping conceal storage

Two cube tables at either end of the sofa and the inverted pyramid coffee table are other ingenious designs custom-made by Boccia. They are designed around empty storage space. The central core is empty, ready to receive whatever odds and ends the client wants to tuck out of sight. To unify the tables with the sofa, their wood-frame structure is upholstered in the same material as the sofa.

The custom-made sofas and club chairs are all low in height. Not only is the low horizontal line restful, it makes the distance from the floor to the ceiling seem longer, giving the illusion of a larger, airier space.

Built-ins add storage space on either end of the radiators

Don't radiators tend to be ugly? Don't walls broken up by windows tend to look choppy? Couldn't we all do with another place to put things? Boccia answered it all by unifying the window walls in both the living and dining areas. He built a deep ledge from wall-to-wall under the windows. Underneath the ledge, on either side of the central radiator, he constructed a storage cabinet. In front of the radiator, he placed a plain panel. Above, in the ledge, he inserted a metal grille to allow the heat to rise as it should.

Above the ledge, pleated solar screen material covers the windows and the wall, unifying it all.

This material filters light and softens the city skyline, giving it the effect of an air-brush painting.

Boccia has truly transformed a depressingly ordinary room into something special.

Sources

Paint on columns and walls: BENJAMIN MOORE. Velvet carpet: ANTRON II/PATTERSON, FLYNN & MARTIN. Sofas, club chairs, side tables, coffee table and columns: Custom designed by THOMAS BOCCIA. All upholstery fabrics: KNOLL INTERNATIONAL. Pleated solar screen drapery: ISABEL SCOTT. Lighting on columns: HALO LIGHTING.

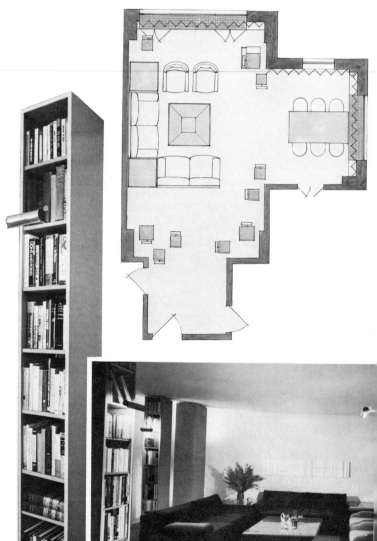

Photos: E. Costa

A STORAGE WALL THAT PIVOTS

Consider the conditions: An ordinary ho-hum apartment. Low ceilings. No architectural distinction. Rooms conveying confinement. The client, a music lover with art objects and a stereo to store.

Enter architect Alan Buchsbaum.

Buchsbaum replaced an immovable wall with pivoting storage cabinets

With one master stroke, architect Alan Buchsbaum gave his client the option of defining his own environment—confined and cozy or open and expansive. Buchsbaum provided storage and display space, and he endowed the apartment with a distinctive architectural ambience. How did he do this?

Buchsbaum tore down the wall between the bedroom and the living room. Acknowledging that his client sometimes loves an open expanse and sometimes prefers privacy, Buchsbaum replaced the wall with units that could pivot to open up the space between the two rooms or close to enclose each room. Although the cabinets appear weighty, they are easy to move. They are made out of plywood and mounted on ball bearings. Lacquered in white, the cabinets are unified with the wall when closed. When open, they contrast dramatically with the parrot green wall beyond and invite passage to this attraction.

Stereo speakers are mounted on the upper part of the end cabinets. (Actually the cabinets pivot only 359°, not 360°. That one degree more would snap the speaker wires.) The upper parts of the cabinets feature shelves for the display of art objects. The bottoms of the cabinets are enclosed, hiding clutter.

The lozenge shape of the cabinets not only looks smooth and sophisticated, it has a practical purpose. The curved corners keep the units from knocking against one another when they are turned.

The handsome steel banding at the bottom and the middle of the units is also selected with more than esthetics in mind. The bottom band functions as a kick plate to prevent scuffing. The middle band unifies the top and bottom halves of the units. (Designing the pieces in two parts solved a practical problem: it allowed them to fit into the elevator.)

In architect Alan Buchsbaum's hands, storage units take on aspects of sculpture and architecture. The soft, rounded shapes and beautiful materials of shiny steel and reflective lacquer suggest sculpture. Because the units act as a wall, and as doors, they deserve architectural attributions. Buchsbaum's is indeed an impressive solution to storage.

Sources

Cabinetmakers: CHARLES COHEN, HARRY VAKASSIAN. Hardware: ELMER T. HEBERT, SIMON'S HARDWARE.

Photography by Norman McGrath

MULTIPURPOSE ROOMS

LIVING ROOM/DINING ROOM/ BEDROOM/OFFICE

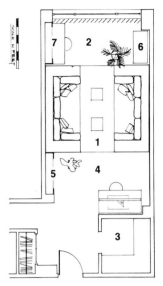

(1) Living, sleeping, reception area (below), (2) office, (3) kitchen, (4) drafting, (5) shelves and bar, (6) stereo, (7) storage.

New York designer Sandra Nunnerley had only a small space, but she wanted to live and work with a sense of style.

Nunnerley noodled on how to reduce the furnishings to the minimum

Beds with their long sides to the walls could work as sofas for sitting. Opposite each other, they would create a conversational circle. Small movable tables could serve as bedside tables and as companions to conversation.

The drafting table would do as a dining table, as a place to spread out a buffet when company's coming. It and a bar should logically be near the kitchen. The bar could be part of a general shelving system.

When it came to the work desk, designer Nunnerley wanted it to be a rather private place, efficient but out of immediate vision. It made sense to place it at the end of the room, farthest away from the entrance. It also made sense to incorporate a work surface into a shelving system similar to that of the bar. After all, repetition creates harmony, and something built in looks like part of the architecture and doesn't crowd the space.

To accomplish her many purposes, Nunnerley custom-designed twin-bedded sofas to incorporate bookcases at the end facing her work area!

Raising the conversational area on a platform zones the room and cuts its length

By raising the conversational area on a platform, the work area would seem altogether more private, the conversational area more expansive, and the dining area more defined.

Sources

Bookcases: CHARLES RULO. Lighting: LUXO LAMP CORP. Foliage: PLANT SPECIALISTS.

Photography by Robert Perron.
Courtesy The Condé Nast Publications Inc.

DINING TABLE DOUBLES AS DESK

Photography by Harry Hartman

The dining room/library combination is an attractive and effective one. The idea certainly suited Marilyn Ruben's clients, a young couple who liked formal dinner parties, but not formal dining rooms. The couple preferred an 18th-century English dining table, a two-pedestal design with an expansive mahogany table top. How could the designer use this table and still make the dining room look like a library? It wasn't enough to push the large table against the wall.

A wall-hung superstructure turns the table into a desk

Designer Ruben created a wooden structure, toned to the table and equal to its length, and mounted it on the wall in a position just above the height of the table top. This ingenious superstructure diminishes the seeming depth of the table and provides desklike cubbyholes and storage spaces within easy reach of the work surface. Clever.

When company's coming and the table takes center stage, the wall-hung structure adapts to the role of a serving surface.

One wall was replaced with a walk-through, back-to-back shelving unit

What is a library without books? Ruben replaced the wall between the living and dining rooms with a walk-through, back-to-back shelving unit. Open shelves on both sides of this storage wall provide space for books, art, and stereo equipment. The enclosed cabinets on the bottom store all manner of other matter. On top of the cabinets one open pass-through area acts as a bar to serve both rooms.

The books—and their colorful covers—lend a cozy informality to the couple's dinner parties.

The lighting can be dim for dinner, bright for reading

To make the room effectively multifunctional, the designer devised a sophisticated system of lighting. Wall washers are recessed into the ceiling. There is a separate switch for the lights on each wall, and each switch is on a dimmer. With all of these light-ing options, the couple can absolutely alter the mood of the room. For their dinner parties, they like to wash two opposite walls in soft light and supplement it with candlelight. When reading, they can direct bright light wherever they want.

Sources

Wall-hung shelf: DESCON WOODWORKING. Dining chairs: 19th-century Queen Anne chairs. Table top: 18th-century Georgian. New table base: ASHLEY KENT. Custom banquette: WILLIAM J. HEINA & SON. Fabric for banquette and walls: KIRKBRUMMEL ASSOC. Rug: STARK CARPET. Cabinet work (bookcases and architectural detail): DESCON WOODWORKING.

THE DINING ROOM AS OFFICE

Even such luminaries as designer Robert Metzger have to make space do double duty. Metzger uses his office as a dining room. For a functional office he needed work surfaces, files, and a lot of storage space for fabric, tiles, wood chips, and other tools of the trade. For his dining room he needed a dining table adequate for a large group of guests, plus storage for linens, silver, and other accoutrements for the table top. In every instance, he wanted the room to convey his own ambience—his design imagination, finesse, and flair.

A center storage island has a fold-and-slide table top

During the workday the table top is about the same width as the cabinets below, with some overlap at the ends. It functions wonderfully well as a work surface and as a way of dividing and organizing working areas. For a dinner party the top folds open to double its size and then slides to balance over the cabinets. Completely open, the table top overlaps the cabinets on all sides, allowing adequate leg space for guests. Using small-scale folding chairs, Metzger can seat four people on each side and one at each end—a total of ten. (The desk areas on the side walls can be used to spread out a buffet. With ten at the table, there's not so much space for serving platters.)

The cabinets below the table top store linens and silver on one side, tile and wood samples on the other.

Functional furnishings are simple and underplayed

The long walls are designed to provide large work surfaces and a great deal of storage space. Long white Formica table tops are supported by chocolate brown filing cabinets, arranged to provide knee-hole desk space for Metzger and his assistants. Wall-mounted storage cabinets and a tall unit of lateral files are colored crisp white like the table tops.

A diagonal-design wallpaper and African accessories create excitement

How primitive and daring. How exciting and sophisticated. How exotic and interesting. Metzger shows his mastery. The diagonal is the most active and exciting of lines and designs. In two tones—brown and white—the wallpaper suggests the primitive energy of a Polynesian tapa cloth as well as the cultivation of a Brooks Brothers herringbone.

The African accessories excite the imagination, as the exotic always does. Another nice touch is the oval crest of the "Consulat General de France." It suggests that those in the know know Metzger. And they do.

Sources

Wallpaper: FIRST EDITIONS. Rugs: HARMONY CARPET. Chairs: PACE COLLECTION. Lighting: HARRY GITLIN. Shades: JULES EDLIN INC. Tableware: DIANE LOVE, INC.

Photography by Darwin Davidson

GALLERY BECOMES A BEDROOM

Photography by Norman McGrath

The kid's in college. Still wants his own room to come home to. The parents want him to feel welcome at any old time.

The parents also had no desire to waste the space in their son's room during the extensive periods while he was away. They did have the desire to display their collection of fine photographs. How is it possible to create a young man's room and a photographic gallery at once?

The boy's mother, Barbara Schwartz, ASID, partners with Barbara Ross in Dexter Design, Inc., was well equipped to seek a solution.

What does a young man need in his room? A large bed. Storage space. A work surface or desk. Room to display and enjoy his hobbies or interests. Durable materials that can take tough

wear. Privacy. Perhaps an acoustically insulated space if he's into playing his stereo at top volume.

What is required for a photographic gallery? Display space. Being able to change exhibits without wrecking the walls. A background that will set off slick black and white photographs. Elimination of glare on the glass-covered surfaces so that one can see without eye strain.

The designers put the bed in a box

A fold-down bed is encased in a 7-foot (2.2-meter) tall box. When the box is closed, it provides four extra walls for the display of photographs. When it is open, one can draw down an extra-length double bed, as comfortable and commodious as can

be. Within the box is a shelf and electric outlets for a reading lamp, a clock, and a radio—everything cozy and convenient.

Walls, floors, and doors are covered in industrial carpet

Carpeted walls don't show nail holes. They hide the evidence of other exhibits. Since the Schwartzes had a large collection of photographs, they wanted to rotate them with impunity.

The soft surfaces provide a pleasing contrast to the hard-edged steel and glass frames of the photographs. The russet color dramatizes the black and white of the photographs.

The continuous coverage of the carpeting serves to unify the room. By avoiding contrast between the walls and the floor, even more attention is drawn to

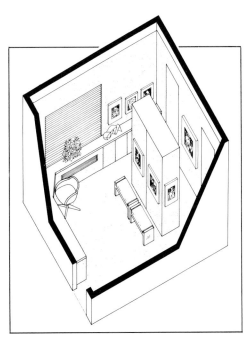

the photographs.

The industrial-quality carpet can take tough treatment. The college student can roughhouse in his room, if he's so inclined. He can also make a lot of noise, for carpeting absorbs sound.

Lighting is carefully controlled

With walls full of glass-covered, steel-framed photographs, glare can certainly destroy comfort of vision. Bright light also brings the danger of damaging the photographs. To control the daylight, the designers hung horizontal blinds at the window. (They selected a silver color to add a shimmer of excitement.) To answer the crucial question of artificial illumination, the designers had the wisdom to consult a specialist. Lighting expert Paul Marantz used a track system with low-voltage spots.

What about the boy's display space for hobbies?

Photography is his hobby and his subject of study.

Sources

Photo display: DIANE ARBUS, series on looking into the lens. Carpeting (industrial grade, viscose/wool/nylon blend): CARPETS OF LONDON. All noncarpeted surfaces clad in FORMICA. Silver blinds: LEVOLOR. Desk chair: HERMAN MILLER. Lamp: CASTELLI ITALIA. Acrylic benches: R & B PRODUCTS. Sheets and pillow cases: BURLINGTON. Track lights: EDISON PRICE. Watercolor: ED BAYNARD. Sculptures: LILA KATZEN. General Contractor: WASCON-BURNS.

Photography by Elliot Fine

BEDROOM ZONED FOR THREE FUNCTIONS

I t started as another boring box, a typical bedroom in an ordinary apartment. Artist Alan Schlussel expected to dress and sleep in his bedroom, but he also needed a place to work and places to store his books and canvases. In addition, he had enough of excitement; he wanted a restful retreat.

Architects Louis Muller and William Murphy offered all the answers.

They built structural divisions within the bedroom to define areas

Two walls and three floor levels define functional areas with the utmost efficiency. Facing the closets is the dressing area—drawers and shelves built into a 9-foot (2.8-meter) wall. The back of this storage wall provides a headrest for the bed and a calming blank wall at the end of the desk.

The entrance to the sleeping area is defined by a raised floor, softly carpeted in beige. The mattress is raised further on a sleeping platform.

In back of the storage wall, the sleeping area is separated from the working area by a 4-foot (1.2-meter) wall. Because the work area is on the regular floor level, the artist can sit at his work table and have an unobstructed view out the windows. From this vantage point, he doesn't even see the bed. Because the wall does not obstruct the flow of sunlight, he can work at his easel with delight in perfect light.

The storage wall has the effect of defining two rooms, each with its own entrance. Enter straight to the sleeping platform. Enter around to the right to the working area. As well as not seeing his bed from the working area, Schlussel is spared looking at his work area while in bed.

The shelves in the storage wall accommodate Schlussel's large collection of books. A saved

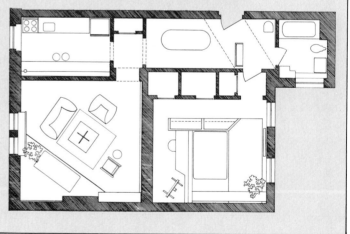

space below the sleeping platform is designed for storing canvases.

A calm, continuous color and minimal furnishings create a sense of serenity

All colors are neutral—cream, beige, café au lait, white. The colors blend together to create a serene sense of unity. Such an unaggressive atmosphere can give one the peace to reach into oneself for creative inspiration.

Minimal furnishings not only

save cluttering the space, but cluttering the mind. This, truly, was the atmosphere the artist was after.

Sources

Wall and floor upholstery: AMERICAN DRAPERY & CARPET. Bedside table: HERMAN MILLER from BUSINESS EQUIPMENT. Hanging light: AIRBORNE/AR-CONAS CORP. Bedspread and pillows: PAUL BROWN. Custom cabinetry: RICHARD L. SANTOS. Luxo desk lamp: HARRY GITLIN.

PART TWO:

FITTING WHAT YOU DO

To make your home comfortable, to make it into an effective support system, it has to accommodate what you *actually* do in your home. Don't make the mistake of designing your home for your fantasies of what you would like to be if only you were the person you wish you were—instead of yourself. I'm reminded of a friend who hired a designer and who was seduced by the designer's image of her lifestyle. The designer thought of my friend and her husband as glamorous young professionals who entertained constantly. My friend didn't dissuade him. She ended up with a "totally taupe" living room and groups of armless chairs—a perfect background for constant entertaining, but no place to curl up to watch Monday night football.

How do you *really* spend your time at home? Cooking, eating, entertaining, doing desk work, reading, watching television, working? Where do you like to do each activity? How do you like to do it? What would be an atmosphere conducive to your pleasure? What would make your activity easier to do, more convenient? Good design can save you time, save you stress. It can also raise your spirits, give you psychological support. A beautiful environment makes you feel good about yourself. When you feel good about yourself, you tend to be more efficient and effective. Look around your home. What doesn't work for you? What can you do to change it into something that will? Sometimes "making do" can drag you down. The cost in inefficiency and depression might not be worth what you save financially. In these days of inflation, it's best to invest in yourself!

More and more people are working at home

Today more and more mothers are making commitments to careers, as well as to motherhood. Fathers, who may have timed their wives' breaths as they delivered, are taking a much more active role in parenting. Long enjoying the pride of providing, they are now finding the fun of nurturing. Shared parenting necessitates more flexibility with work schedules. Many are finding the solution by setting up offices at home.

Futurist Alvin Toffler, author of *Future Shock* and the more recent *Third Wave*, projects that we'll be working from "electronic cottages." Connected with the world through our own home computers, we will no longer have to crowd into the cities, the subways, the airless elevators to get our work done. We can hook up from home. Home is becoming more and more a professional workplace.

Designing the home as a professional workplace, as well as a place to relax and tune out the tensions of the day, is quite a challenge. How do you make the same space work both ways? Changeable lighting, movable furniture, softening the office image are some solutions.

The best design solutions to working at home come from a focused consideration of the nature of the work and what would make it most comfortable and convenient. A film producer's townhouse incorporates a projection tower for a dozen or so projectors and an illuminated cabinet for slide editing. A dancer's loft has "building block" furniture that can be moved out of the way for exercising or arranged for living. A suburban design team cut skylights in their attic and opened the area to the floor below to give their new work place a sense of space and an air of inspiration. A Minneapolis stockbroker chose furnishings that spelled success and a way with wealth—an image to convey confidence to his clients. A professor of English at UCLA, who loves The Royal Shakespeare Theater, built a stage in his home so he could entertain the troupe and be entertained as well. There is no set formula for working at home. You can work at whatever you want and make whatever you want work!

The kitchen has become a social center

Cooking and eating have become more important in our lives. Better educated and better traveled, today's generations are interested in the cuisines of the world—and in trying them out at home. More aware of health and proper nutrition, we are more selective about the foods we eat to keep fit. It's still true that we need to eat to live, but no longer are we willing to make this functional fact the end of it. By imagination and artistry we can transform the experience of nourishing ourselves into an exquisite pleasure. Something beautiful, sensual, sensational can nourish our eye, our view of life's bounty, our sense of our own worth. Food can nourish our souls, as well as our bodies.

We're having more fun with food in an era when most of us have less time than ever to prepare it. With more and more women working outside the home, we rely on modern technology to cook quickly. (The microwave oven and the Cuisinart are examples.) Women also rely on other members of the family to make meals. So cooking time has become social time, a time for the family to get together and swap tales of the day. Friends also get in on the act. They too contribute to the cooking and join in the chopping and cutting up in the kitchen.

Cooking has become a social activity, fun for all.

Because the cook wants company in the kitchen and because everybody seems fascinated with food, the current kitchen has become a larger, prettier place. Architects making renovations usually tear down the walls of the pantry, the maid's room and bath, and the connecting corridors to make one big open living space. With guests increasingly being invited into the kitchen, the kitchen itself has become more of a showplace.

There is often an eating area incorporated into the kitchen, either a counter with stools or a separate dining table with chairs. Dining areas are often only separated from cooking areas by an island or partition that conceals the clutter of cooking, while still encouraging communication with the cook.

To allow variations in mood—from efficiency to intimacy—lighting is designed to be varied. Task lighting for work counters is often fluorescent tubing mounted under cabinets. (Be sure to choose fluorescents in "warm white" to make your food look appetizing, not rancid.) Incandescent lights on dimmers are used to provide warmth and intimacy in the eating area.

A beautiful kitchen isn't for guests alone. It can help inspire the creativity of the cook. One woman desired a celestial space (maybe to help her pastries rise), so she covered one wall with a blue-sky mural. French chef Lydie Marshall evoked the atmosphere of France with white stucco walls, a Breton armoire, French tiles, and copper pots. Chinese chef Jim Lee put shoji screens on his ceiling. City-bound but longing for the country, actors Ann Jackson and Eli Wallach decorated their kitchen with wood planking on the walls, quarry tiles on the floors, and straw baskets on the shelves. To inspire your own culinary artistry, use whatever turns *you* on.

Eating and entertaining in the kitchen seem to be a celebrity style, according to Certified Kitchen Designer Florence Perchuck. The informality and warmth of the kitchen encourage intimacy, a sharing of personalities rather than platitudes.

To save time and effort, the actual cooking area is engineered for efficiency

To save steps, it is ideal to have major appliances no more than 4 feet (122 cm) from each other. A triangular arrangement of stove, sink, and refrigerator is the most efficient. Counterspace adjacent to each appliance will help coordinate the look—and the cook.

Often-used equipment is within easy reach, maybe kept on open shelves or in cabinets above the work space, maybe hung from the wall or from an overhead pot rack. Chef Lydie Marshall keeps her wire wisks and cutting boards beside the stove. Chef Saul Krieg keeps a frighteningly vast collection of knives for boning, carving, and decorative cutting in wooden knife racks along the walls.

Everything should be engineered for the convenience of the cook. A short person might want work counters to be especially low; a tall person could save back problems if counters were higher than usual.

What kind of cooking goes on in the kitchen? Special needs can inspire special designs. Chinese chef Jim Lee cleans five pounds of shrimp at a swat. The shelves under his sink are used to store scouring powder and the usual stuff, but they also pull out to become a bench where two can sit comfortably together to clean shrimp. For baking, Lee explains, dough won't get soggy on cool marble. So for his own baking preparations, Lee uses the marble top he removed from a friend's old bureau. Chef John Clancy stretches strudel over his stove. He covers the gas burners with an acrylic cover. (The pilot light is electric, so the burners can be covered without causing a fire.) For his baking equipment, Clancy has a drawerful of tin and aluminum molds, all separated into sections by acrylic dividers. (The form for a baba au rhum should not get mixed up with that for the barquette or brioche.) Chef Saul Krieg keeps all coffee machines on the counter itself. He, like many of us, needs all the help he can get in the morning.

The kitchen has a multifunctional future

Kids have long been coming to the kitchen to play under mother's watchful eye. Family members who in the past have tended to make foraging forays to the kitchen to snatch a snack or to peek in the pots tend now to stay, to sit down to visit, or to pitch in with the preparation. Guests, who once darkened the door only when desperate for ice cubes, are now invited in for dinner. Yes, the kitchen is a social center, but it is more.

In some homes the kitchen has merged with the family room. In addition to the eating space, there is sitting space, both for lounging and for watching television. Ron Carter, an owner of a video production company in Los Angeles, uses *his* kitchen as a multimedia viewing room.

The kitchen is often an office, with desk top, files, and drawers located conveniently by the telephone. This convenient center for planning and ordering is bound to be updated dramatically by today's technology and that of the future. Like television, and the telephone before it, the home computer is destined for popular usage, even though most of us today consider its use in our own homes a rather strange idea. Our own mini-HALs of the future will help us buy bargains, do our taxes, add up our calories or cholesterol, monitor our home's energy consumption, and in general get organized. The kitchen is bound to be the mission control center where we can play with computer puzzles while waiting for the water to boil.

No longer is the kitchen a soulless Siberia for overworked, underpaid labor. It's the social, emotional heart of the house. In the future, it may be its brains as well.

How do you like to entertain?

Do you like to have friends over? What do you like to have them over to do? Do you like to have large cocktail parties? Sit-down dinners? For how many? Maybe everybody plays pool in the basement, or the kids play dress-up in the attic. Make a list of what really goes on or of what you'd like to do. Your home can be designed to accommodate whatever activities you prefer.

If you're fond of cozy conversations, remember that it is impossible for more than six or eight people to carry on one conversation. Arrange your seating groupings accordingly. If you like to have large cocktail parties, design your space so people will have room to stand and to move about. If some enchanted evening a guest at your house sees a stranger across a crowded room, you better make it possible for him to fly to her side! (Assuming, of course, that neither is your spouse!) If you like to give dinner parties, how many do you want to invite? Provide sufficient seating space. Expandable tables are often a good bet, and you can keep extra dining chairs in the bedroom or use them in the conversational circle.

For mood making, you can create allure for the eyes and ears. A spotlight can focus on a beautiful art object. Room lights can be dimmed to suggest softness—mystery, romance. Music can soothe the soul or excite the spirit. All these changes can be made at the flick of a switch.

Entertain yourself

Don't make your guests more important than you make yourself. A lot of people seem to leave their large living rooms deserted except when there's company. Even then, they take their close friends into the kitchen or some other more relaxed room. It is not necessary to repeat the lifestyle of your ancestors if it's not really the way you like to live. You might redesign that large living room to make it more informal and relaxed so that *you* can enjoy the space. For formal occasions, put on a clean shirt. The people who like you, like you the way you are. And if they don't, who needs them anyway? (If you *do* need them for business or some other serious reason, find a compromise that allows you to please yourself. Ironically, sometimes the most formal and stiff people seem to allow themselves to relax and have a good time if you do.)

In this chapter you will see how homes have been designed to accommodate the activities of specific individuals. Designers have saved their clients' time by making their activities more efficient, more comfortable and convenient. They have raised their clients' spirits by making the atmosphere surrounding those activities something the clients perceived as beautiful and inspiring. Consider how you spend *your* time. Your home too can be designed to enhance the time of your life.

WORKING AT HOME

How do you create a friendly place for the family to relax and still project a professional corporate image? Designers Judith Kovis Stockman and Lee Manners of Stockman & Manners Associates, New York, faced this problem when designing a producer's townhouse. The 14 x 18-foot (4.3 x 5.5-meter) family living room was to be the professional screening room for presentations to clients. It had to work as a place to edit and select slides and to orchestrate accompanying music. It also had to be home—a place to relax and tune out the tensions of the day. How did the designers do it?

The designers created a free-standing projection tower

Judith Stockman explains: "It was obvious that the most visible of all elements, the projection tower, had to enhance the space, it had to become a sculptural element that would perform while not being obtrusive during non-working hours. We decided to insert the projection tower into the existing architecture of the room as a full-height, full-width volume which would float free of walls and ceiling. Continuous incandescent lighting between the architecture and the tower as well as the tower's clean, glossy finish separate it from the more ornamental quality of the architecture."

At night, the lighting around the edges makes the monolith seem like a free-floating sculpture. The lighting directs the eye away from the projection equipment. The projection tower actually incorporates an incredible amount of equipment. Storage behind the tower hides carousels, tape recorder, turntable, and supplies. Projector and dissolve equipment are wired to a programmer at the control center. Each shelf can be adjusted for precise projection.

A triangular cabinet for slide viewing hangs along one wall

A triangular cabinet, housing illuminated slide-viewing boards, is hung along the wall opposite

A PRODUCER'S WORKSPACE WITHIN A FAMILY LIVING ROOM

Photography by Ed Stoecklein

the fireplace. When closed, the cabinet becomes an unobtrusive, but interesting, sculptural shape. It casts a pleasing light down on the plants on the shelf below it, creating a relaxing and intimate atmosphere.

The simple L-shaped sofa provides plenty of seating for five in the room's limited space. Its base and back are carpeted like the floor. The cushions are removable, so that the slide editor can stand on the base to get a good look at the slides she's editing.

Large, simple shapes, calm colors, and effective accent lighting project both the professionalism and the intimacy desired in this small working/living space.

Sources

Construction: KURT BARENS-FELD, SEGOVIA CONSTRUCTION. Carpet installation: ARDEE FLOOR COVERINGS. Cushions: FOAM-TEX. Fabric: M.H. LAZARUS & CO. Projection light: LIGHTOLIER. Core lighting: WIREMOLD CORP. Painting over fireplace: RICHARD HESS.

CLEARING THE DECK FOR DANCE

Lynda Rodolitz was not up for fussy furniture. She needed an open expanse in which to express herself. She selected her New York City loft for the floor—the open area where she could videotape, act, dance, do what she loved to do. Furniture would only get in the way. However, since this place was also her home, Lynda Rodolitz needed a place to sit down, a place to rest and relax. She needed storage for her books and personal effects. How could she get the comforts of home while still preserving her space? Designer Tim Button of Stedila Designs orchestrated the answer.

Movable building-block furniture provides seating and storage

Whatever furniture impeded the flow of the floor had to be movable. Tim Button designed the furniture with polystyrene skids so it could easily be pushed against the wall, out of the way.

The furniture needed to be large, grand in scale, in order to be suitable to the space. Yet grand furniture may not be easily moved. Instead of designing one big bulky piece, Button achieved a grand effect with building blocks. A 4 x 8-foot (1.2 x 2.4-meter) upholstered base provides a surface for seating; its open end provides a place for books. A red lacquered wooden block atop creates a backrest for the seating and storage on the other side. Seat and back cushions combine for comfort. The building-block units can be changed and rearranged at will. One upholstered base is topped with a wedge. Combined with another base, the surface provides a fine place for exercising or relaxing. Other units are organized into an eating area. This area is differentiated by peach, instead of pink, upholstery.

Photography by Robert Perron

To raise the seating to dining height in the eating area, Button added another layer of cushions. These he colored in a tone deeper than the base to emphasize his layered look (see lower left).

The consistently rich red lacquered backrest/boxes throughout the space add up to an amazing total of 100 feet (30 meters) of shelving. In this loft, both dancer and designer are masters of saying something in space.

Sources

Furniture frames: PANNER WOODWORKING. Upholstery fabric of quilted moving pad material: RENNERT MANUFAC-TURING COMPANY, INC. Upholsterer: BRUCE SHENTON.

SUBURBAN ATTIC HOUSES DESIGN TEAM

It wasn't working. The office off the bedroom was just too dark and small to accommodate the husband and wife design team of Shelly Rosenberg/Design Studio. What to do? Well, there was an unfinished attic above. Something might be done with that stuffy space.

Skylights and an opening to the floor below made the attic an airy aerie

The designers cut two windows into the slanting attic wall, built a large skylight over their old office, and located another smaller one over the interior attic bathroom.

They removed the attic floor over their old office so that it would have a sense of soaring space and a sunny exposure to the skylight and so that the attic would lose its sense of confinement. By opening the attic to the space below, the whole area seems to flow. The attic becomes a pleasant perch, a place where you can feel on top of the world.

The new attic office was designed for a sense of space

Walls were painted glossy white to reflect the light. Wall-to-wall gray industrial carpeting unifies the space and makes it look businesslike. Built-in storage and seating make the most of the space while keeping it uncluttered. There are drawers and storage slots along the long wall, a closet and a deep cabinet for drawings and blueprints on the end window wall, and a wall-to-wall platform sofa for guests and clients on the other end. Furniture out in the open space is light looking. There is a drawing board and stool, a wicker chair and pale pine coffee table to go with the sofa, and a Formica work table in an architectural green grid design, along with two green chairs. So simple and professional.

Notice the details. Behind the deep cabinet for blueprints is a triangular mirror—seems like another window opening out. The plants and touches of green also serve to connect the indoors with the outdoors. As a wall ornament, there is a capital of a col-

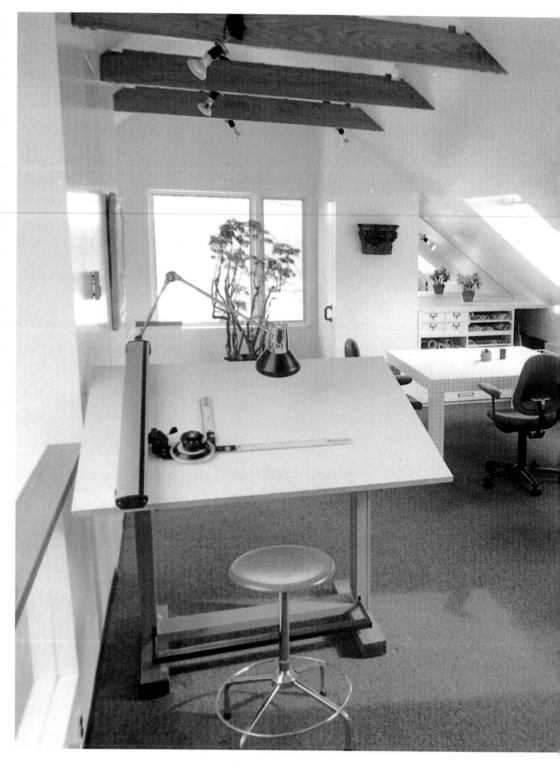

umn—a reference to the designers' expertise with architecture.

Having created such a pleasing place to work, the designers converted their old office into a reference library. They even brought some of the sunshine into their master bedroom by cutting an opening in the wall

between the bedroom and library.

These designers certainly knew how to open up the pleasant possibilities of their suburban home. By breaking through the roof, the floor, and the wall, they created a sense of sunshine and space.

Sources

Paint: PRATT & LAMBERT. Carpet: STRATTON INDUSTRIES. Files: SUNAR. Drafting table and chair: HERMAN MILLER. Breuer chair: ICF. Desk top: FORMICA. Upholstery: ASTRUP CO. Vertical blinds: LOUVERDRAPE.

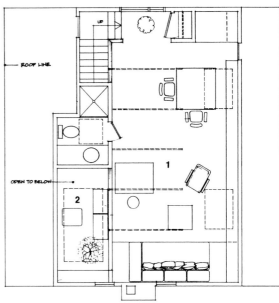

(1) New office, (2) former office (top photo), now library.

Photography by Shelly Rosenberg

AT HOME IN THE EXECUTIVE SUITE

The Minneapolis stockbroker wanted to work from his home. He wanted the place to inspire his clients with confidence, indeed an eagerness to put their money in his hands. He also wanted to make the place into a comfortable home for his family and friends. Michael Tedrick of the Lexington, Kentucky, design firm of Lloyd & Tedrick did it all.

Conservative colors are used in a daring way

Nothing unusual about cream, white, and brown used in combination with an Oriental rug. Here, the designer expressed the stockbroker's knowledge of the right combinations, *and* his derring-do, by putting the dark color on the walls. Covering the walls in deep, warm mink-brown excites the imagination and creates the cozy illusion of a cave—a safe place, something like a vault—but warmer.

Furnishings are classics of good taste

If certain furnishings symbolize status, objects that those in the know would want and admire, this apartment has a selection with wide appeal. No matter what one's prejudices of period, there's something here that you're likely to like.

Textures are rich, sensuous

Everything is so downright sensuous that it would be impossible not to feel attended to in this place. The secretary's office contains all the normal business equipment, but the harshness of the typical textures is softened by luxurious materials. Office filing cabinets, colored the mink-brown of the walls, are organized under the windows by a wall-to-wall topping of travertine.

The office looks like a library

The broker's office is designed to be comfortable, unthreatening. The furnishing style is more ordinary, middle of the road. The walls here are cream; the sofa style is a Lawson. There are family photos on the wall. The room oozes confidence and comfort.

Sources

Herez rug: STARK CARPET. Louis XV armchairs: reproductions by YALE R. BURGE, covered in a BRUNSCHWIG & FILS fabric. Fretwork sofa table, Chinese ca. 1800, imported by LOUIS D. FENTON. Barcelona table, Charles Pfister corner sofa upholstered in sueded leather: KNOLL INTERNATIONAL. Screen, attributed to late 18th-century North Asia: RIFFEMOOR ANTIQUES. Brass and chrome reading lamps (adjustable): CEDRIC HARTMAN. Oriental vase (ca. 1800) table lamp:

FRANK KAY ANTIQUES with shade and wiring by SIEGMAN-AMBRO. Grayed-tan wool gaberdine window treatment: CENCI.

Chaise (or Recamier): a Michael Tedrick design, manufactured by KNOLL INTERNATIONAL, upholstered in a CLARENCE HOUSE cotton matlasse. Sofa pillows: Oriental rug fragments from KARL MANN. Pedestal for tusk

sculpture by Anthony Redmile: INTREX. Parsons table: INTREX. Table cover, Ashanti tribe pattern of gold and silver on ecru cotton: FORTUNY. Brno chairs upholstered in sueded leather: KNOLL INTERNATIONAL. Elk horn and silver chandelier by ANTHONY REDMILE with hand-crocheted string shades by SIEGMAN-AMBRO.

(Bottom, left) Study/office walls are covered in natural raffia basketweave by KNEEDLER-FAUCHERE. DUNBAR's Lawson-style sofa covered by BORIS KROLL fabric. Window treatment: THORP & CO. Carpet: "Tenerife" pattern by PATTERSON, FLYNN & MARTIN.

(Bottom, right) Secretary's office. Desk: MCGUIRE. Open arm

chairs: JOHN MASCHERONI, upholstered in CENCI fabric. Chesterfield sofa: DUNBAR, upholstered in KIRK-BRUMMEL linen velvet. Chinese ancestral portrait: KARL MANN. Wire base table with marble top: KNOLL INTERNATIONAL. Woven Wilton carpet: "Petronius" by JACK LENOR LARSEN.

ALL THE WORLD'S A STAGE— EVEN THE LIVING ROOM

When he talked to the architects about building his home, the bachelor professor of English at UCLA explained that he likes to play host to The Royal Shakespeare Theatre during their visits to Los Angeles. And in his new home he wanted to provide the troupe with a stage! The professor's home was designed for drama under the direction of Charles Moore by the Los Angeles office of Moore Ruble Yudell.

The fireplace focal point is center stage

The fireplace is used as a sculptural space divider. Vertically, it separates the two-story dining room from the two-story living room. Horizontally, it connects, by a bridge, the guest room and the small study on the second floor.

It also creates a proscenium stage. It is a recessed backdrop. Scenic banners, creating theatrical illusions, could be hung over it from the balcony above. Openings on either side of the fireplace and end both of the balcony provide actors with all manner of possible entrances and exits.

A lighting grid is mounted above the doors, opposite the fireplace

A grid of metal tubing, accommodating wiring and electric outlets, faces the fireplace/center stage. Spotlights can be mounted wherever wanted. Gels and other emotion-evoking lighting equipment are easily accommodated. The light-supporting structure extends out of doors as well, framing the patio where drama can be presented alfresco. (It's a nice touch that the tubing of the grid echoes the shape of the balcony balustrade.) Good show.

Sources

Fireplace tile: MAX BOISSAUD.

THE KITCHEN AS SOCIAL CENTER

KIBITZING OVER COCKTAILS

Designer Bob Van Allen likes company when he cooks. The kitchen of his Manhattan loft is designed so some can kibitz comfortably over cocktails, while more ambitious others can roll up their sleeves and join in the chopping, pureeing, and preparing.

A long butcher block counter (with storage underneath) provides plenty of space for the cook and his helpers. A laminate-clad peninsula jutting out from the work counter, attended by hard-edged banquettes lined with soft pillows, keeps the others comfortably close for conversation. Although the banquettes have the presence—the seeming solid-

ity—of architecture, they glide easily in and out of position. Furthering the unity, and the architectural aspect, of the composition, overhead lighting is housed in a rectangular box that repeats the shape of the table.

When Van Allen entertains on a larger scale and wants more formality, he hires outside help and closes off the kitchen by lowering Levolor blinds. The peninsula then acts as a serving area for a larger white dining table accompanied by mellow English antique chairs.

Sources

Blinds: LEVOLOR.

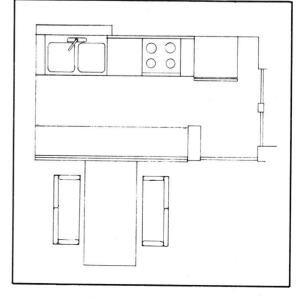

KEEPING COMPANY WITH THE COOK

The owner of this kitchen not only wanted to show off his kitchen to company, he wanted to show off his company with his kitchen. Affiliated with Copco, he wanted a place where the company's new cookwares could be photographed for promotional purposes.

Sensibly, he hired Barbara Ross and Barbara Schwartz, ASID, of Dexter Design in New York to do the job. To set off the Copco cookware, they selected rich materials in neutral colors.

To organize the space to work well for the client's own personal pleasure with friends and family, they tore down part of the pantry wall to open up the kitchen and to create a bar adjacent to the living room. The cooking area is kept comfortably compact in an area raised on a platform. A radius-edged counter connects the platform area with the lower level. Company can watch the cook in action or take part in the

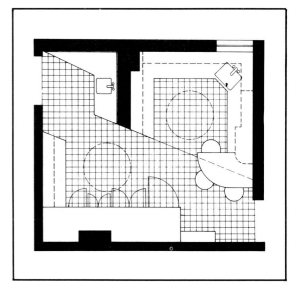

preparation while seated on a stool. (To compensate for the difference in level, the stools are of different heights.)

Sources

Lighting: LIGHTOLIER. Cabinets: ROSELINE PRODUCTS, tops and faces surfaced in brushed chrome and pumice FORMICA. Blinds: FLEXALUM. Tile: AMERICAN OLEAN TILE.

COMMUNAL COOKING

Country airs

The kitchen is a center of social activity for the young, globe-trotting couple who live in this Connecticut home (builder LuAnn DeGenaro). Guests who come to dinner often get involved in its preparation. Ample counter space allows room for a community of cooks. A serving counter, 6 inches (15 centimeters) higher than the work surface, provides a convenient place to pass along food to the dining area, while at the same time keeping the clutter of cooking out of view.

Located on the second floor, with large windows and an adjacent deck, this cooking/dining area has the airy openness of a treehouse. To echo the outdoors, architectural designer Christopher Woerner of Stony Creek, Connecticut, chose surfaces of wood. To preserve the open feeling, he avoided eye-level storage cabinets and relegated such equipment to an adjacent pantry.

Lighting over the working area is serviceable fluorescent. To allow the couple to create a mood of warmth and intimacy when they're entertaining (or when they're alone), other lights are incandescent and on dimmers.

Celebrity style

Ann Jackson and Eli Wallach get rave reviews for their dinner parties as well as for their acting. Whether catered or prepared by them, all meals are cooked and served in their Manhattan country kitchen. Certified Kitchen Designer Florence Perchuck explains: "They wanted the kitchen to serve as an entertainment center. We converted four existing rooms into one open-plan space with a center island, a food preparation area flush with the wall, and an adjacent dining area."

Perchuck adds that it seems to be a celebrity style to entertain in the kitchen. In this particular kitchen, congenial warmth and intimate informality are communicated by wood planking on the walls, country-style wooden chairs, Mexican tiles on the backsplash, quarry tiles on the floor, and copper pots and straw baskets.

Sources

Cabinets: SVP KITCHENS & BATHS (Perchuck's firm). Wood-paneled walls, columns, and dado: CHAMPION BUILDING PRODUCTS. Quarry floor tile: AMERICAN OLEAN TILE. Mexican backsplash tiles: ELON. Counter tops: CORIAN by DUPONT. Lighting: LIGHTOLIER.

Photography by Robert Perron

Taking the heat off the cook

If you are lucky enough to own a beach house, you'll probably want to invite friends and family to come and enjoy themselves, but you'll sure not want to spend *your* vacation working every minute to prepare meals. The kitchen in a beach house should encourage community cooking!

This simple, clean scheme does. A wall-to-wall counter covered in white tiles provides an extensive work surface. The island opposite, incorporating a sink, gives someone a fine spot for washing fresh vegetables and doing dishes. With the dining table only a few feet away, a person at the sink can still have the pleasure of a congenial conversation with those sitting at the table. With the L-shaped conversational area still in sight farther down the room, the cook is in a fine position to holler for help.

Open shelving over the stove keeps much-used equipment within easy reach and keeps company from asking, "Where is. . .?" Closed cabinets along the side wall conceal objects not used every day.

Architect Carl Hribar kept all elements low, both to encourage a relaxed feeling and to add to the cool air of openness.

Sources

White tile surfaces: AMERICAN OLEAN. Floor, platform, and table base: MAGEE flat industrial grade carpet. Tubular incandescent lights on dimmers under shelving: LUMINLITE. Hanging lamps: ABOLITE. Chairs: SCANDINAVIAN DESIGN. Range: JENN-AIR.

Photography by Elliot Fine

Photography by Studio Nine

Fun with food

Who said, "Don't play with your food!"? Why not? Food is what cooking's all about. Cooking certainly is a central activity of any kitchen, so why not focus on food as a decorative theme? And why not have fun with it?

The cabinets in this kitchen have gathered some crop of vegetables! They are invitingly larger than life. Painted over custom cabinetry by artist Lester Gaba, the mural provides a fun focus for this family's favorite gathering place. Notice how the dishtowel overlaps the edge. The artist was playful too. For fun in fooling the eye, he asked the cabinetmaker to specially detail this area.

In a Manhattan brownstone, this kitchen was created from what the architect/owner Ken Ross calls a gutted "rabbit warren." The food preparation area was designed for efficiency, with flush-mounted appliances and counters under the cabinets and a work island opposite.

On the other side of the island is the dining area. Enhancing the eaters' enjoyment, the height of the island hides the cooking area from view.

For extra richness in esthetic effect, counters and backsplash are covered with warm red travertine. Lighting contributes to the mellow mood. A ceiling spot focuses on the mural. Dimmable fluorescent strip lights under the cabinets (concealed by an aluminum strip) illuminate one work surface. A ceiling-mounted light box over the island floods the other. This kitchen certainly is a tasteful treat.

Sources

Travertine: FARO MARBLE CO. Cabinets: Custom, fabricated by SLG FURNITURE, Sink: AMERICAN STANDARD. Cooktop: THERMADOR. Appliances: GE.

Functional fun

The kitchen should be an informal, cheerful place, efficient and easy to clean. This kitchen has it all.

A Formica mural backs up the eating area. The design spills down onto the floor, continued in tiles. The design incorporates an open area that provides a pass-through from the kitchen cooking area and a visual/verbal connection with the cook.

In a 19th-century downtown Savannah home, this contemporary kitchen is completely new. When the owners moved in, they found the kitchen in a wood lean-to structure added to the original building. Restoration architects Robert Gunn and Eric Meyerhoff felt the owners would lose nothing by lopping off this addition and making way for a contemporary kitchen. Designed in an efficient L-shape, the kitchen features cabinets with built-in appliances as well as storage space.

Sources

Range, oven: GE. Laminated plastic: FORMICA. Flooring: CENTER BROS. INC. Sink: KOHLER. Dining chairs: THONET. General contractor: BRAUN CONSTRUCTION CO. Carpentry: WOODCRAFT CABINET & HARDWARE CO.

Photography by Robert Perron

Let the sunshine in

Located on the crown of a high hill in Westchester County, New York, this spacious new house has a kitchen that capitalizes on the view. The window wall (at the right of the photograph) connects with a trellised terrace—a wonderful place for relaxing and feasting the eyes and taste buds. Sunshine and slatted shadows penetrate the kitchen, enhancing the cook's pleasure in his/her place of business. Architects Stern & Hagmann enhanced the sense of sunshine by surfacing the center island in Formica of a yellow hue. To contribute a further feeling of comfort and warmth, they chose easy-on-the-feet, easy-to-maintain gray carpeting.

So the owners could close off the kitchen or open it up to the dining room, the architects fitted an opening on the end wall with a special garage-door-type track. The door can roll down or roll back up into the ceiling.

Photography by Ed Stoecklein

Sources

Kitchen contractor: WEST-CHESTER CUSTOM KITCHENS. Carpet: HARMONY CARPET. Laminate: FORMICA. Oven: THERMADOR. Range: ROPER. Sinks: ELKAY. Lighting: EDISON PRICE.

DESIGNING FOR EFFICIENCY

The magic triangle

There is a "magic triangle" in kitchen design. It is ideal to have the major appliances 4 feet (1.2 meters) from each other so you can spend your time cooking, not commuting. It is perfect to have counter space between the appliances so that you have convenient places to work and set things down.

This kitchen was once broken up into three separate areas. The owners knew they were dissatisfied with their cramped quarters. They hired Charles Morris Mount, a gourmet cook who specializes in the design of kitchens. Mount recommended tearing down the walls and making one big kitchen out of the three small areas. He recommended scrapping the old cabinetry and appliances and making a fresh esthetic, efficient start. To use the space the best, he suggested covering two viewless windows with cabinetry.

To achieve the "magic triangle," Mount arranged appliances along two adjacent walls and in a center island. The four burners on the island are easily accessible from either side.

Having covered most of the windows, Mount was concerned with proper ventilation. He specified a red round hood for over the burners. It ventilates at three speeds, one "strong enough to dry hair," he quips.

To give an airy aspect to the enclosed room, Mount chose surfaces in smooth white Formica. The floors are natural slate. The butcher block top of the central island and the dramatic red vent overhead add warmth and excitement to the fresh new working/living space.

Sources

Cabinets: ROSELINE, surfaced in FORMICA.

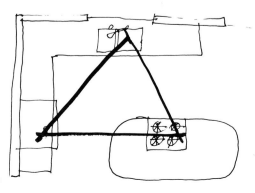

Her cooking is heavenly

Another maxim of kitchen design is to make things comfortable for the cook. The cook in this kitchen is a petite woman who likes baking bread. Her architect, C. T. Long, installed a butcher block bread table at an unusually low height to meet her need for kneading.

Notice also that a selection of spices is at the end of the counter. This makes the mixing of various concoctions most convenient. No rummaging around in deep, dark drawers.

An overhead pot rack, echoing the shape of the counter below, puts pots and most-used baskets within easy reach. Other utensils are arranged on the wall by the kitchen sink, easy to grab at a moment's notice. It is clear in this kitchen that good design can save time.

Not only can a kitchen fit our size, accommodate our activities, and save us time, it can soothe our spirit. A sky mural on one wall, with puffy cumulus clouds and a suggestion of a rainbow, evokes a celestial space. In this kitchen, more than the coffee is heavenly!

Sources

Mural: MICHAEL D. BOOTH. Pot rack: Custom design by architect C. T. Long, fabricated by PIVOT DESIGN SERVICES, INC.

Photography by Robert Perron

MAKING THE MOST OF THE OLD

The cabinets in this kitchen were the original 1940s units found in the house. Nicholas A. Calder of Dramatic & Different Designs, Ltd., in Greenvale, New York, gave them an updated look. He stripped their surfaces, lacquered them a Chinese red, and fitted them with simple metal pulls.

The light fixtures above were created from gutted fluorescent fixtures. They were redesigned to accommodate food-flattering incandescent lights, brass plated on the inside and enameled red on the outside.

To set off the excitement of the red, the designer covered the walls with black acrylic sheets. The narrow corridor kitchen, once a conventionally depressing place, attains the upbeat tempo of an adventurous evening out on the town. Furthering the glamorous aura of his creation, the designer placed mirrored window boxes under the large windows to magnify the sparkle of the light.

Sisal matting covers the floor and the L-shaped banquettes that define an eating area at the end of the room. The banquettes are designed with flip-top seats so that storage can be secreted underneath. Combined with the shiny red and black, the natural sisal gives an additional exotic Oriental accent to the space. A black dining table by the banquettes and red and black patterned pillows on them unify the composition. (Imagine what you could do if you were daring!)

For more formal dining, there's a dining room through a swinging door at the other end of the kitchen (see plan).

Sources

Accessories: MARIANO STUDIOS, FOUR SEASONS. Art: RHODA OCHS GALLERY. Black linen table: CAROLE GRATALE. Black and red fabric: ALADIRE. Ceiling paper: WALLTRENDS. Acrylic walls and étagères on top of counter: NITA DESIGNS. Carpentry, acrylic installations, brass countertops: VOGUE ENTERPRISES. Lighting: STEVE LIGHTING & DESIGN. Oriental fabric window shades: KIRK-BRUMMEL. Cooktops: CORNING.

Photography by William Rothschild

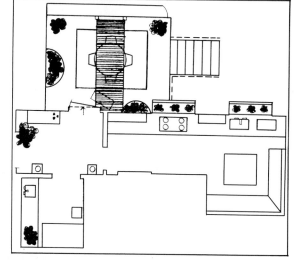

Photography by Elliot Fine

19TH-CENTURY CHARM WITH 20TH-CENTURY EFFICIENCY

The floors were beautiful—oak parquet with borders of walnut and cherry inlaid in geometric patterns. The windows were special too—framed with handsome wooden moldings, with top panels of luminous stained glass. The 19th-century Brooklyn brownstone had a lot of charm.

The owners wanted to preserve the charm of their home while still making their lives convenient and comfortable. Their architect understood the problem. David L. Hirsch of Bier Baxt & Hirsch, New York, believes that in renovations the kitchen is one area that must be completely rethought.

To create an efficient working space, he created a peninsula with an island opposite. The peninsula incorporates the sink, plus butcher block counter space. The island opposite incorporates a range with a countertop that not only provides working space but an overlapping area for eating.

The island is arranged on the diagonal to make the most of the space and to show off the wood border of the floor. Since the kitchen was to be used as a family gathering place, the diagonal also defines a play area on the other side. The parents can putter with the cooking while still keeping an eye on their toddlers romping around.

A bright red Formica-clad vent over the range eliminates smoke and odors, keeping the kitchen a pleasant play space. A sharp-edged triangular shape, the vent hood slashes the space and emphasizes its openness.

By covering counters, railings, and edges of shelves with warm wood, the architect echoed the beauty of the Victorian oak floors. Cabinets are clad in easy-care white Formica, providing (and communicating) contemporary convenience. A planter niche in back of the sink allows plants to be placed where they complement those in the corner diagonally opposite—another confirmation of the diagonal dimension.

For variations in mood, lighting can be altered. For a soft, suggestive effect, it can come down solely from the venting hood. For allover brighter light, there are fixtures recessed in the ceiling.

Sources

Cooking units and ovens: CHAMBERS. Refrigerator: AMANA. Sink fixtures: KOHLER. Baffle down spots: LIGHTOLIER.

WORKING OUT A SMALL SPACE

The owner loves to cook and wanted an expansive space in which to enjoy his creativity, but he was stuck with a small, narrow kitchen. What to do? He called in Richard Mervis of Richard Mervis Design, New York.

"The narrow counter [see pictures top right] functions as an extra workspace and as a fold-out breakfast surface for two," Mervis explains. "The cart unit (middle pictures) pulls out to reveal a large butcherblock cutting surface with drawers and vertical tray storage below. It can be wheeled everywhere in the kitchen, but is most convenient next to the stove." At the end of the counter, "a niche [bottom, left] houses shelving for cookbooks and a small desktop near the telephone. The mirrored bar [bottom, right] in the pantry was originally a closet."

"My main objective," Mervis affirms, "was to create the most serviceable kitchen possible out of a rather awkward space." He succeeded.

Sources

Cabinetry: GIB SMITH. Lighting: LIGHTOLIER. Laminate surfaces: FORMICA. Floor: FLEXCO. Appliances: SEARS. Chairs: DESIGN RESEARCH. Bronze mirror at bar: HILLSIDE GLASS.

THE FUTURE NOW

Ron Carter, owner of a video production company, wanted his kitchen to function as a media room, as well as a most modern kitchen. To realize his dream, Carter collaborated with designer Byron Savage of Savage-Price Company of Beverly Hills. Savage began by eliminating some walls. In the open area he created, the designer accommodated food preparation in an efficient corner arrangement faced by a cooking island. The cooking island features the revolutionary Fasar range that has no flames and no obvious burners. A round cutting board in the corner of the L-shaped section (see plan) covers a disposal chute which goes right to the outside trash can. No longer does the man have to take out the garbage. (This is a definition of manhood that men have never liked anyway!)

For Carter's multimedia presentations, Savage created a large carpeted platform backing the cooking island. Plush leather chairs are arranged for comfortable viewing of the Advent screen. White plastic chairs, drawn up to the cooking island, provide a place for eating, while enjoying the show. Also, with its unobtrusive Fasar cooktop, the top of the island works well as a service center to the viewing area. Please pass the popcorn.

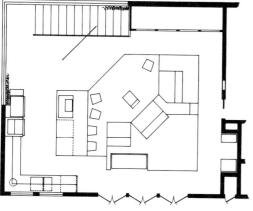

Photography by Giovanna Dal Magro

Photography by Balthazar Korab

EXPANSIVE ENTERTAINING

What are you working for anyway? The people who live here wanted to have *parties.*

They bought lakeside property in Oakland County, Michigan. Together with architects Tobochman and Lawrence of nearby Birmingham and interior designer Florence Barron, they designed the new home with expansive areas for entertaining.

The large living area is designed in four friendly parts

No matter how many people you entertain, it's impossible for more than six to eight people to carry on one conversation. Besides that, no one entertains *all* the time. Home has to be comfortable without company.

The designers divided the enormous 31 x 50-foot (9.5 x 15-meter) room into areas. An Oriental rug defines a grouping in the center section of the room.

An open-sided chaise opposite the central sofa completes the central conversational circle, but it does more. It creates a connection between the central conversational grouping and two L-shaped conversational groupings at the lakeside end of the room. Each of these L-shaped arrangements can seat from six to eight people.

The dining area is placed in back of the central sofa and defined by another large Oriental rug. Matching mirrors and buffets to the sides dignify dining with service and symmetry. Tall plants by the buffets suggest a psychological division of the dining and living areas.

This home bespeaks a celebration even before the ice is out of the refrigerator!

Sources

Four-seater sofa, a Ward Bennett design for BRICKEL. Lamps: CEDRIC HARTMAN. Dining chairs: PACE COLLECTION. Dining table: custom made. Modular seating: PACE COLLECTION. Acrylic coffee tables: DAVID BARRETT.

GLITTERING ENTERTAINMENTS

For most of us, this apartment is a fantasy. On the 49th floor of a multiuse midtown Manhattan skyscraper, the apartment has simply spectacular views. The wealthy international official who uses this apartment gave his designers a budget in excess of a half million dollars, and then left town. By trans-Atlantic cables he communicated his wish to have a contemporary and elegant ambience and a place to entertain his friends and associates when he was in town. Martin Hertz and Thomas V. DiCarlo, AIA, of Shepard Martin Associates, New York, delivered the goods.

Separate seating areas allow flexibility in entertaining

The large living room features two groups of seating. One, in plum, is comfortable for a small group of four or five. Another, larger grouping composed of an L-shaped modular seating system and an upholstered banquette could convene a conference of international officials. Open areas between the groupings provide plentiful standing and circulation space for large cocktail parties. The separate dining room has a view as inspiring as that from an airplane window but here one assumes that the food is better.

The spectacular city lights inspired the design of the apartment

The unquestionable attraction of the city's glow and glitter as seen from the full-height windows inspired the designers to echo the attraction with variable lighting.

They wrapped the modular seating L with custom cabinetry designed to radiate illumination from the top and/or the bottom. The lighting on the bottom creates a floating feeling, a wonderful weightlessness suitable for this 49th floor. The illumination above can nurture plants or show off art objects.

Throughout the apartment recessed incandescent lights in the ceiling are on dimmers so that the master of the house can manipulate the mood as he wishes. The dimmers are built into control panels in each room. These panels also contain controls that serve to tune the quadrophonic sound equipment and adjust the motorized draperies. Talk about having control!

Lighting is used cleverly at the entrance as well. A marble pool with gently gurgling waters serves to introduce guests to the serenity of the space. The water, its floating lilies, and the healthy hanging plants are illuminated and enhanced by lighting recessed in the ceiling above. Black louvers hide the fixtures and soften the effect. Mirror to the side of the reflective pool gives a glittery glisten—an appropriate invitation to enter this elegant apartment.

Sources

Dining chairs: KNOLL INTERNATIONAL. Dining table: APOLLO. All custom woodwork: CREATIVE WOODWORKING. All wallcoverings: WOLF-GORDON. Table in entrance gallery: APOLLO. Oriental runner at entrance: THE GHIORDIAN KNOT. Modular seating: SORMANI. Cocktail table: SAPORITI ITALIA. Custom upholstery: MANNO UPHOLSTERING. Fabric: JACK LENOR LARSEN, INC. All carpets: PHOENIX. All draperies: DRAPERIES FOR HOME AND INDUSTRY. All sound systems: SONIQUE SOUND SYSTEMS. Plum sofa and lounge chairs: HELIKON.

Photography by Ernest Silva

PART THREE:

THE NEED FOR A RESTFUL RETREAT

After the day you've put in, don't you deserve to go home and relax? Don't you deserve a little pampering, a little pleasure? Don't you *need* some refreshment in order to gather your forces for the challenges of tomorrow? All of us need to regroup, to rest and refresh ourselves in order to be at our best. A nurturing home is a powerful force in helping us fulfill (and enjoy) our potential.

I used to live in a fourth-floor walk-up that depressed me. I stayed there because it was cheap. Finally I couldn't stand it any more. The man across the hall was throwing his girl friend out in the hall in the middle of the night and she would ricochet against the wall at the head of my bed. The guy upstairs would come home at 3 A.M. and loudly replay the jazz gig he had just performed in some club on Long Island. And in the apartment with the bathroom that shared the wall with the side of my bed, someone was vomiting. I moved just in time to save my mind.

My new apartment had a fountain (instead of garbage cans) in front, a doorman with a snappy uniform, and an elevator—which was a good thing since I selected an apartment on the 23rd floor. I decorated the new apartment just the way I wanted, instead of making do with what I could get cheap or free. I can't tell you the difference the new apartment made in my psychological set. I woke up in the morning with the feeling that I had something going *for* me, instead of against me.

How can you make your home into a place of refreshment?

Where were you happy?

You might begin by imagining a place where you were once utterly happy. Close your eyes and imagine. See what images come up before your mind. The image that comes to my mind is the beach in the moonlight. All those shimmery silvers on the soft rolling water. There's something about that tide rolling in and out that makes me realize that the fate of the world doesn't depend on how I resolve my current crisis—whatever it is. The world will go on, and I'll probably survive. Since moonlight on the water helps me unravel and relax, I used moonlight on the water as the design theme for my apartment. I covered the dark entry hall with silver Mylar wallpaper and did the rest in blue, silver, and white. Now I feel refreshed at home.

It would seem that Elizabeth Williams is happy when out in the country, gazing at the sky. Everything in her apartment evokes the boundless freedom of the open sky and the cozy comfort of country living. Where were you when you felt most in harmony with the world? How would you describe that place? Write down the words that come to mind. How can you suggest those feelings, those colors, those sizes and shapes, those hard/soft, smooth/rough textures in your home?

What's your heritage?

Remember coming home from school or college and being comforted by the familiarity of your old room? Maybe with your new sophistication the room seemed childish to you, but it was still your own special place.

A friend of mine told me his parents moved when he was at college. When he came home on vacation to see his family, it didn't feel like home. His sister had a bedroom of her own, and of course, so did his parents, but there was no bedroom that was his. He had to sleep on the fold-out sofa in the den. Nothing was familiar, nothing was his. He felt emotionally abandoned.

There is enormous comfort in familiarity. Maybe you want objects in your home that suggest your past. Familiar objects somehow seem accepting. They've seen you at your best and worst, and they're still hanging around. They seem to accept you as you are and be supportive. They give you a sense of belonging.

Of Spanish heritage, Adela Holzer hired a designer also of Spanish heritage, Rubén De Saavedra. He intuitively understood what would make Mrs. Holzer feel at home. In the special "spa" he designed for the family, he worked with bright, clear colors and tiles suggestive of Spanish/Moorish architecture.

You don't really need to have the literal objects of your past. You can, through clever design, evoke the atmosphere of your past. Then you can enjoy both the comfort of familiarity and the self-esteem of pride in your past.

What is it that you like about your house?

What is the architectural style of your home? What is it about that style that's appealing to you? Maybe you identify with the era of its invention. Maybe the spirit of those times is something akin to your own.

Designers Mindy Gross and Michael Harris were hired to do the interiors of a Tudor-style house being built in Los Angeles. What was their client after? What was it that he liked about the Tudor style? Did he identify with Henry the Eighth? The designers psyched it out. Imagine Henry the Eighth in his rich robes eating a mutton chop with his bare hands. Their client was after a feeling of earthy elegance. To fit the feeling, the designers selected large simple furnishings of rich, natural materials. The client got exactly what he was after.

Is your home late Colonial or Georgian? Maybe you like a feeling of refinement and formality. Do you live in a ranch house? Maybe you chose it because you like to live in a relaxed, informal style. Maybe you were attracted to the rambling romance of a Victorian house. If you can identify what it is about your house that appeals to you, you can choose furnishings that have the same sort of appeal. The furnishings will have a natural harmony with the home—and with you!

What are your favorite furnishings?

Even if you live in a totally nondescript house or apartment (like a large percentage of us), there's still hope for inspiration. Do you have any favorite furnishings? Treasures from your travels? Old family heirlooms? A special collection you've gathered over the years? An unusual painting, picture, poster? You can design your home around the objects you love.

Designers Joseph Minicucci and Jerome Hanauer had a client living in an oh-so-ordinary New York apartment. Of course this special person wanted her own home to be special. The designers used her old family Oriental rug as the focal point of the conversational circle and her collection of blue and white porcelain as important accents all through the apartment. In the entry hall, they painted the walls blue, set up the porcelain on shelves of white and lit up the display with ceiling track lights. They made the most of their client's treasures, and the apartment became a totally personal place.

Your favorite furnishing, if large, can become the center of attraction or focal point of a room. Smaller objects can be gathered together for added impact. Any favorite object can inspire your color scheme. You can make your whole home as likable to you as your favorite object.

Curved shapes take the edge off; soft textures mellow the mood

You can translate the feeling you're after into the language of design. If you're after relaxation, curved shapes seem less stiff and rigid than straight shapes. Straight shapes, like a soldier at attention, suggest discipline and control. Curved shapes suggest natural flowing forms—like flowers or how you look curled up with a book in bed. Curved shapes that are soft are especially relaxing—like a big, rounded-arm overstuffed sofa. Soft things, like carpet, upholstery, or even fabric-wrapped walls, absorb sound, making a place more calm and comfortable. The jarring noises of the outside are *kept* outside. In addition to absorbing sound, soft textures seem to insulate. They seem to keep the temperature more comfortable for us. Difficult to relax when you're freezing or sweating to death. Lovely to relax when the temperature feels good on your skin.

Soothe your mind by being good to your body

Speaking of skin, today we seem to be taking better care of it than before. The skin and the body inside. Even glamorous magazines stress good health as the best beauty aid. Good circulation that comes with exercise can make your face look younger. Exercise and proper diet can add years to your life, and so can the reduction of stress!

What better way to relieve stress and relax your muscles after the tensions of the day than to take a long languorous bath? With more and more women working outside the home during the day and having to manage the household business in less and less time, the pressures to perform are incredible. How can a woman handle it all? She can do better for others by taking the time to take care of herself.

The bathroom is a place to retreat, to be alone, to relax, and to re-

fresh oneself. It is no longer simply a utilitarian space to be used with embarrassed alacrity. It can become a personal paradise.

Terence Conran, known for his household shops here and in Europe, has a sofa and writing table in his family bathroom. This secluded private spot is a place to gather one's thoughts, as well as to bathe. Flowers add a sensuous scent to the room.

Pleasure to the senses eases the tensions of the mind. Imagine escaping the winter weather, traveling to some tropical isle, and soaking your body in the soft, sun-washed water. Ahhhh! Who cares about anything else? All those troubles at home don't seem to matter much any more. This is what's called "getting perspective." Sometimes you have to get away from a problem in order to see what it is and how to handle it.

Going to the bathroom down the hall is clearly a less expensive trip than traveling to a tropical isle, but it too can soothe your senses and give you perspective. Some people actually design their bathrooms to simulate a favorite vacation spot. In one couple's home, her bathroom looks like a Grecian garden; his suggests an African safari. A beautiful bath is not a licentious indulgence. It's an investment in the good life—yours.

Zoning the home for public and private places can make it more livable for all

The bathroom doesn't need to be the only place where you can get away from others. Additional accessible escapes make living with others a more pleasant proposition. Even children need places free from the intrusion of others. Why do you think they find hiding places under the beds where no adult could possibly enter? What do they find so alluring about tree houses? Why do teenagers long for their driving licenses? Everyone needs a peaceful place where they can be away from others, where they can gather wool or their thoughts or just not do anything.

A person's bedroom seems to be a private place, while the dining room, living room, and kitchen seem to be areas of communal activities. In a Palm Beach apartment used by a Chicago couple for winter weekends, designer Donald Paterson tore down the walls separating the living room, dining room, and den to make one big open space for pleasant parties. The master bedroom with its dressing room and bath is closed off for perfect privacy. And so is the guest suite. A vacation house on the Italian Riviera, designed for a family of three generations, features sliding doors. They can be opened when the mood is convivial and closed when the mood is contemplative quiet. To recognize that at times all of us have the need for others, and at times we don't, can help us organize our homes with both public and private places. A home that can accommodate our real needs can indeed be a restful retreat.

Design with an eye to easy maintenance can save time and effort

When time is precious, who isn't bored with spending it cleaning? It pays to purchase materials that are durable and/or easy to clean. The object will look better longer, and without spending time fussing over it, so will you! It's particularly important to choose easy-to-maintain materials in a vacation home. After all, it's particularly grating to spend vacation time cleaning! Wet-washable floors, such as ceramic or stone, are also cool under the feet in a hot climate. Plastics, vinyls, laminates, Formica are a boon to the cleaning contingent. Fabrics that can be thrown in the washer save children, dogs, and other pets from feeling guilty. A true home is designed for people's pleasure, not for museum tours.

A whimsical surprise can relieve your home of the weight of earnestness

The designers of that Tudor house in Los Angeles thought that the interior was getting too heavy and serious, so they put a bright red tractor stool in the bathroom. For her daughter's bathroom, designer Jeanette Longoria used an old copper tub she found in a Mexican market. Unusual objects, found objects, something initially designed for another purpose—anything serviceable, but surprising, can give your home a light touch. Surprises are fun.

CURVED SHAPES TAKE THE EDGE OFF

On edge? Want to come home to rest and relax? Most of us, after making an effort all day, want to come home to a place that gives us an unchallenging sense of support. Stanley Felderman, a skilled designer who completed the famous corporate offices of Fabergé before he was 26, well understands the executive's need for rest and revitalization. Now heading his own firm, Stanley Felderman Ltd. Design Group, and working with partner Allen Felsenthal, Felderman shows in this Park Avenue apartment how to create a soothing space.

A predominance of curved shapes softens the space

Lozenge shapes, rectangles with rounded ends, define areas of the apartment. In the entrance foyer, fabric-wrapped rounded columns contain a center section of floor-to-ceiling mirror. A curved wall in back leads the way to the powder room.

Up two steps to the living room, the same lozenge shape is repeated in mahogany with a center section covered in fabric. A mahogany bridge over the top conceals lighting focused on a painting. You'll notice that this lozenge shape doesn't go up all the way to the ceiling. The designer used this shape to divide the long living room into living room and den. In back of this lozenge are bookcases serving the den.

Still standing in the foyer, but looking to the left, you'll see another mahogany lozenge shape. This one defines the difference between the foyer and the dining area. Here the center section features shelves of glass, which set off a crystal collection.

Acting as room dividers, the lozenge shapes become elements of the architecture. Echoing the architecture, furnishings have a predominance of curves. The dining chairs are Louis XV in style, with curved tops and legs. Even the rectangular dining table has curved corners. Notice the occasional chair upstairs in the living room. The seat and back are both soft and curved in shape. Notice too the curved band bordering the living room rug.

Turn the page and you'll see that the coffee table and end table have fun with circular shapes. The end table lost a piece of its pie, and it looks like the coffee table gained one.

Curved elements predominate in the den and kitchen too. A curved wall in the den abuts the bar. In the kitchen, a raised eating area features a round table and curved banquettes backing to a curved counter. Overhead, a curved cabinet echoes the shape of the counter. Ceiling soffits incorporating lighting also sculpt the space with curves. Hardly a sharp edge in sight.

Soft textures and pale colors further mellow the mood

All the walls in the living and dining rooms, the halls, and the master bedroom are wrapped in fabric. The raised living room area is covered in carpet. Draperies at the dining room windows are designed to fall in soft folds rather than sharp pleats. These soft textures provide a comfortable contrast to the shiny glamour of mirror and glass, as well as a foil for the dramatic brass ceiling over the foyer and dining area.

Pale colors—whites, creams, and naturals—are the dominant colors of the apartment. They set off the dark tones of the mahogany dividers. The pale colors and rich woods together convey a look of luxury—inviting at the end of the day.

Sources

Shelves, cabinet, and brass ceiling: TEKLETS WOODWORKING. Wallcovering: LEE/JOFA. Dining table, buffet, coffee table: BOZZANNO WOODWORKING. Dining chairs: CORVIN CHAIRS, covered with TRESSARD FABRICS. Dining banquette: FINE ARTS, covered with STROHEIM & ROMANN fabric. Lucite sculpture above dining table: LES PRISMATIQUES.

Living room carpet: C.J. ZIMMERMAN. sofa: FINE ARTS, fabric by JACK LENOR LARSEN. Avon side chairs: FINE ARTS, fabric by LEE/JOFA, STROHEIM & ROMANN. Cylinder end table: PACE.

Bar in den: TEKLETS WOODWORKING. Four-part table in den: ARTHUR BECOFSKY. Kitchen shelves and cabinets: TEKLETS. Kitchen table, TV stand, and work surfaces: ARTHUR BECOFSKY. Cabinet hardware: FORMS & SURFACES. Tile: HASTINGS TILE. Cabinet lighting. ZAK ELECTRIC. All flowers: ED STIFFLER.

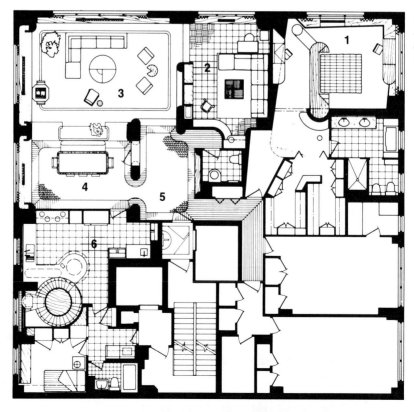

(1) Master bedroom, (2) den, (3) living room, (4) dining room, (5) foyer, (6) kitchen.

WHERE WERE YOU HAPPY?

Photography by Robert Perron

One secret to designing a home that makes you happy is to begin by imagining a place where you were once utterly content and happy. Think about that place. Get its image in your mind. What are its colors? Its shapes? Its symbols? Believe it or not, you can use the same colors, shapes, and symbols suggestively in your home to recreate the same sense of well-being that you felt in your favorite place.

Ever lie on the ground, looking up at the sky, watching the clouds go by? Did you feel a wonderful sense of serenity, a sense of peace and pleasure with the world? One would guess that Elizabeth Williams did. Her duplex Manhattan apartment does everything to evoke a lazy afternoon in the country, a sense of sunshine on the skin, a sense of the airy openness of a boundless blue sky.

Elizabeth Williams knew what she was doing. A Parsons graduate and a trained designer (now into a career in film editing), Williams worked with her architect friend Ted Long, a city planner with a large architectural/engineering firm, to recreate the atmosphere of her favorite place in her own apartment.

A little bit of heaven

Knowing they were after an open effect, the designers began by stripping the apartment to its bare bones and removing partitions between rooms.

To suggest the sky, they painted the ceilings blue. In the kitchen the effect is even more explicit. One wall is covered with a mural of the sky, complete with clouds and a rainbow (see page 63).

To create a floating feeling, the designers suggested sky below as well as sky above. In the living and dining areas, oiled parquet floors are covered with

faded cotton Dhurrie rugs in pale blue and white.

In between, furnishings seem to float like clouds. Softly shaped seating in the living area is covered in bleached patterns of yellow—white washed in sunshine. Much of the furniture in this area actually *is* floating. Upholstered pieces, pillows, and ottomans can be moved by whim (if not wind). Only the round-armed sofa is stationary.

Metal étagères between the living and dining areas have a light look, and like the wings of an airplane, they catch the glint of the sunshine in the open space.

The fireplace focal point in the living area contributes enormously to the celestial scheme. Surrounded in space-expanding, light-multiplying mirror, the fireplace features an enchanting free-floating soft sculpture called "Cloud Ladies" by quilter Elsa Brown.

The dining area opposite features its own space-and-mind-expanding focal point, a large canvas by artist George Lahey.

Some country calm

To suggest a sense of the country, Williams and Long used natural wood and wicker, as well as plenty of plants. The mantel at the hearth is of honey-colored oak. It blends beautifully with the baskets holding firewood and kindling. The fireplace surround is of ceramic tile, in a delicate design of blue on white—a traditional country look. In the dining room, the table is wood, the chair seats and backs are of woven wicker, and so are the baskets decorating the walls. In bedrooms upstairs, hand-crafted quilts contribute to the cozy country feeling.

The timeless traditions of the country and the endless openness of the sky combine in this individual's apartment to create

an everyday atmosphere of cozy comfort and boundless freedom. Elizabeth Williams has taken a once-felt sense of well-being and turned it into her constant environment.

You could do it too. Imagine your favorite place. Write down the words that the place suggests. Then figure out how to translate those words into furnishings that will express the same feeling. Fantasy *can* become reality!

Sources

Soft sculpture: "Cloud Ladies" by ELSA BROWN. Fireplace tiles: COUNTRY FLOORS. Fabric: CHINA SEAS. Bedroom wallpaper: HINSON. Bedroom side chair: M. MITTMAN. Dining room mural: GEORGE LAHEY. Dining table: SMITH AND WATSON. Dining chairs: STENDIG. Dhurrie rugs: STARK CARPETS. Etagères: ABSTRACTA. Wallpaper: WOODSON.

WHAT IS IT YOU LIKE ABOUT YOUR HOUSE?

The client was having a Tudor-style house built for himself in the Ramirez Canyon area of Los Angeles. He hired his designers while the house was still under construction, and his only instruction was that he preferred an "English country" look.

What were the designers to make of that? English country can mean anything from chintezes with cabbage roses to family heirloom antiques, to just a well-seasoned look of shabby splendor. What did the man mean?

The architecture of the house provided a clue. What was it about Tudor that appealed to this person? Think of Henry the Eighth padding around in his palace. There was a look of luxury all right, but it was rough and ready. Earthy elegance.

The designers psyched out the situation. They didn't go around searching for Tudor oak antiques. They gave their client the feeling that felt good to him.

Mindy Gross of Mindy Gross Interiors, Los Angeles, and Michael Kurt Harris, now with his own firm, The Design Corps in Los Angeles, collaborated with each other and their client to actualize his unspoken dreams.

Furnishings are few, large in scale, and luxurious

Henry the Eighth had large rooms and few furnishings. The modern master of the house got the Tudor style all right, but interpreted in small-size rooms with tall ceilings. To keep the space uncrowded and to provide a presence sufficiently grand to match the ceiling height, the designers chose few furnishings, but ones massive in size.

With its big brick fireplace, rough plastered walls, and wooden beams, the home conveys a feeling of earthy energy.

Photography by Robert Stein

Furnishings too were chosen in rich natural materials. Furniture shapes were also chosen to echo the architecture. Choosing furnishings compatible with the size, shape, and texture of the architecture is a sure way to achieve harmony.

Unexpected surprises delight and excite

"The house was beginning to look too serious at one point so we added a few things to lighten it up," the designers explain.

Additions include a bright red tractor seat in the bathroom, a soft, serene Oriental screen in the bedroom, with other Oriental touches and modern graphics throughout the house.

Harris concludes: "When you're out in the hectic world all day, it's very important psychologically to come home to balance and quietness. Home should be a sort of 'safe place.'"

Sources

Dining room English oak table: KNEEDLER-FAUCHERE. Dining chairs: WICKER WICKER WICKER. Wood bowl: NEW MANILA IMPORT CO.
Living room upholstered furniture: DONGHIA, upholstered in channel quilted cloth by GRETCHEN BELLINGER. Pillows: JACK LENOR LARSEN. Coffee table and sconces: DENNIS AND LEEN. Foyer console and vase: DENNIS AND LEEN.
Master bedroom (left): Chair, ottoman, pillows: DONGHIA. Fabrics: GROUNDWORKS. Bedspread: SHOWROOM III. Table: DENNIS AND LEEN. Bathroom (top): Terrazzo: DEL PISO. Rug: STARK. Tractor stool: ICF. Second bedroom (opposite): Hand-painted screen: WILLIAM GATEWOOD. Table: BAC STREET. Chair: WALDO'S. Lamp: PALACEK IMPORTS L.A. Shades: CONRAD IMPORTS.

Photograph from Terence Conran, *The Bed and Bath Book.*
Courtesy Crown Publishers.

BEHOLD THE BATH

The bathroom is much more than just a place where you wash. It is a place to be alone—to get away from others. A place to rest and relax and commune with yourself. A place to renew and refresh.

Treating your senses with sensitivity is one wonderful way to make yourself feel good. A long, languorous soak in warm water can relax your muscles after a long hard day. A vigorous rub with a fluffy towel can stimulate your skin. Lotions can brace your face or smooth your skin.

Whether small or large, your bathroom can become your own personal paradise. Colorful towels, mirrors, candles, flowers, pictures—any or all can contrive to make your bathroom an especially personal place.

Terence Conran, known for his household shops here and in Europe, has made his own home's bathroom into something special. A large space, the room accommodates a comfortable sofa, a writing desk, and even a working fireplace. Imagine sitting in the sunshine, inhaling the sensuous scent of flowers while writing personal notes. The room inspires a relaxed harmony of body and mind. It's a refreshing retreat.

THE ULTIMATE INDULGENCE

On target

"It is my personal philosophy that bedrooms and bathrooms are vital as individual sanctuaries. Unfortunately, they are underplayed or overlooked by many designers. I always start a project there and design out." Charles Burke, a talented young California designer, practices what he preaches in his own home. In his sunken circular tub, he is at the center of his universe. A circular wall mural above the tub shows that he's on target. A circular window (cut from reclaimed closet space) on the adjacent wall further emphasizes his intention. A yellow brick road leads to the luxury of the bath. Its edges are enhanced with inlaid lighting. (Called Tivoli lights, the tiny bulbs encased in clear plastic tubing are imbedded and grouted into the floor tile.) For additional pleasure and privacy, there are 14 separate lighting controls, overhead heat lamps for drying, security monitors, and capability for future conversion to a steam room. Built in the late 30s, Burke's Los Angeles house certainly has an updated feeling, which sustains the drama of the Art Deco era.

Photography by Max Eckert

Sources

Tile: INTERFACE. Fixtures: KOHLER. Gold ball light sculpture: SONNEMAN. Tivoli lighting: CHARLES BURKE.

Photography by Otto Baitz

A feeling for wood

In an upstairs corner of an angular house he designed in Connecticut, architect Robert Nevins provided a pleasant place for dressing and bathing. Having a strong attraction to the warm earthiness of wood, he surrounded the space in cypress. With bathing areas oriented to the seascape of Long Island Sound, the wood provides a comfortable contrast. For serviceability, cabinets and closets are covered in plastic laminate. Actually brown in color, the laminate seems to take on the tones of the sunlight. Cypress strips, used for handles on the cabinets and closets, unify the units with the vertically paneled walls. Mirrors are placed to multiply the pleasure of the ocean view.

Sources

Tile: blue-green glaze on terra cotta. Custom woodwork: HOMEWOOD CABINETS. Plastic laminate: CONSOWELD.

Photography by Robert Perron

Plastic fantastic

"I ask my clients to choose what fantasy environment they'd like to live in—Hollywood, a space ship, Tahiti...," confided a straight-faced Robert Shaw. The writer who inhabits this tiny bathroom obviously opted for tropical paradise. To transform the ordinary bath into a flight of fantasy, Shaw began by leveling the walls. He installed sheets of masonite above the existing tile. Over this smooth surface he affixed sheets of plexiglass with a tile adhesive. The tropical design in green plexiglass he cut and applied on site himself. A clear acrylic shower stall opens up the view to the tree. A suspended ceiling, also sheathed in green plastic, has light above that is directed to wash the walls and create the illusion of sunrise or sunset. "Plastic is really the best material for the bathroom," Shaw asserts. "It is impervious to water, sound-proof, and won't scratch if properly cared for and scrubbed with nonabrasive cleaner."

Sources

Fixtures: AMERICAN STANDARD. Plexiglass: AIN PLASTICS.

FANTASIES IN THE BATH

Photography by William Rothschild

Light fantastic

Mirrored walls and sparkling ceiling lights transform a tiny powder room into a splendid space. Measuring only 5 x 5 feet (1.5 x 1.5 meters), the room suggests something as grand as Versailles. Marcus Caine and Ed Mayerson of Mayerson, Caine, Inc., Springfield, N.J., are responsible for this magic.

Sources

Black onyx vanity: SHERLE WAGNER. Wilton carpet: STARK. Stainless lighting tiles: LIGHTOLIER.

Photography by Allen Carter

Grecian garden and tiger's den

These are hers and his bathrooms. Not hard to guess where each likes to spend lazy hours. Her bathroom has the classic purity of Greece. His has the exotic excitement of Africa. For this client couple, Mexico City designer Arturo Pani created distinctly individual retreats for refreshment.

The Grecian garden is an oval room, with floors and tub of marble. The woman can relax in the oval tub and absorb the room's cool sense of serenity while gazing out at the garden through the classic columns.

The man, a hunter, can dream of the excitement of safari. He sits in a sunken tub patterned like a tiger's skin. (It is actually made of hand-set mosaic tiles.) The sink is set into a richly carved wooden table and mirrors above fold out from carved wood paneling. The room's rich textures inspire with earthy excitement.

Photography by Alexandre Georges

Nouveau riches

The clients wanted to make their modern bath into something special, personal for them. Ascertaining that they were fond of the flowing natural forms of the Art Nouveau style, designers Bleemer, Levine & Associates of Miami commissioned craftsmen to carve woodwork according to accurate drawings of that period. Now framed in richly carved bleached oak, the dressing room creates a pleasing and personal contrast with the marble-clad tub room. Mirrored closet doors open from their outer edges to form a three-way looking glass.

Source

Carpeting throughout: EDWARD FIELDS.

Photography by Allen Carter

Fun with found objects

The copper tub was found in a Mexican market. An artist gussied it up with jaunty stripes. Faucets for it were fitted right into the wall. An old wash stand became the vanity. Other found objects, a French mirror and Art Nouveau sconces, complete the scheme. All is set off with mirrored walls. This wonderfully whimsical bathroom was designed by Jeanette Longoria for her daughter Jennifer. No need to serve conventional needs in conventional ways. Serviceable surprises can delight the eyes and lift the spirit.

HOW CAN YOU TAKE AWAY THE TENSIONS IN YOUR MIND?

The tensions in your mind build up in your body—make you stiff and inflexible, less able to relax and enjoy. You can work out the tensions in your mind by working out the tensions in your body. Exercise can not only make your body beautiful, it can free your mind—allow you to focus and have fun.

Adela and Peter Holzer are busy, productive people. She is an author, a producer, and a dealer in heavy machinery and automobile parts. He is a cargo shipping magnate. With the pressure of their days, Adela and Peter Holzer need to relax. They wanted a "health spa" in their home.

They called on their favorite designer, Rubén De Saavedra, and asked him to build an addition to their weekend retreat in New Jersey. De Saavedra had already designed the couple's townhouse, country house, office, and yacht. They knew he would know what they wanted.

A "health spa" at home

With architectural assistance from Richard Thomas, De Saavedra designed a wonderful place to relax and rejuvenate. He added a new wing to the house and oriented it to face the Olympic-size swimming pool. The pavilion provides a focal point for the pool, as well as practical convenience. Adela Holzer, an ardent swimmer, can come right in for a sauna and/or steambath.

In the center of the pavilion, facing the swimming pool, is a cold-plunge pool. A giant conch shell mounted on the wall over it drips water into the pool. De Saavedra is sensitive to the soothing sound of falling water. At night, the conch shell is illuminated. Its intriguing natural shape, reflected in the shimmering pool, provides a romantic focal point for night swimmers—suggestive of far-away places.

On the right side of the pavilion is the gym. A physical fitness enthusiast, Peter Holzer knew what he wanted. Specific exercise equipment was selected according to his specification. For comfort and quiet, the wall against which the equipment is mounted is carpeted.

On the left side of the pavilion is the massage room. The room also serves as a lounge and occasionally as a guest room. Behind the lounge is Mrs. Holzer's Ja-

cuzzi room. A wonderful place to get warm in the winter, the room is red. Red vinyl walls and red tiles on the floor set off the sumptuous white Jacuzzi, as well as the scenery through the upper-level windows.

A dressing room adjacent is the opposite. Walls and floor are white; the bench, bright red. The room presents a cooling effect to a person emerging from the sauna.

Materials are chosen to evoke the client's heritage

It's often comforting to evoke the images of childhood. Of Spanish origins, Mrs. Holzer feels relaxed and at home in an atmosphere suggestive of her heritage. Of Spanish heritage himself, Rubén De Saavedra knew the impulse and the imagery. The colors he chose are bright and clear. The reds, greens, and blues are full of vibrancy and vitality. A predominance of tile not only makes the pavilion easy to wet-wash, it suggests Spanish/Moorish architecture, as does the dripping conch shell. To ornament the outside of the pavilion, De Saavedra chose hexagonal tiles that are antique pieces from Portugal. By incorporating references to his client's heritage, De Saavedra has designed a spa in which to lift spirits, as well as weights.

Sources

Hexagonal 18th-century Portugese tiles: OBJETS PLUS. Vertical blinds: HOLLAND SHADE. Wall-coverings throughout: WOLF-GORDON WALLCOVERINGS. Floor tiles: COUNTRY FLOORS. Massage room bed frame: TUSCAN WOOD ART. Coffee table and planter: INTREX. Wall lights: HABITAT. Painted throw pillows: RUBEN DE SAAVEDRA. Oil painting: LALE.

Ceramic face in Jacuzzi room: OBJETS PLUS. Painting in Jacuzzi room: MAXINE FINE. Dressing room bench: INTREX. Lighting fixtures: HABITAT.

Antiqued steel panels over cold-plunge pool: FORMS & SURFACES. Carpeted wall in gym: "Tretford" carpet by ROSECORE. Gym equipment: MAC LEVY PRODUCTS CORP. Suspended lighting: LIGHTOLIER. "Pedrito," lithograph by BOTERA. All plumbing hardware and door-knobs: PAUL ASSOCIATES.

Photography by Daniel Eifert

FOR WONDERFUL WINTER WEEKENDS

The winters in Chicago get mighty cold. What better way to spend a long winter weekend than in one's own apartment in Palm Beach, Florida? Donald M. Paterson had clients who wanted to do just that. They found a penthouse apartment in a Palm Beach highrise and then left it to Paterson to turn it into a wonderful weekend retreat.

Off with the overcoats—those weighty wools and furs—and on with the bathing suits. The Florida sunshine melts the ice in the veins and encourages relaxation and fun with friends. In their apartment, the couple wanted private places to rest and unravel. They also wanted an arena for exuberant entertaining. And they didn't want to worry at all about upkeep or maintenance.

Paterson tore down walls to make an open area for entertaining

Initially the living space was broken up into dining room, living room, guest room/study, and balcony (see plan). Paterson removed the dividing walls (indicated by dotted lines on the plan) to create a great big open L-shaped area for entertaining. People can flow freely through the space, finding friends, food, or drink.

Donald Paterson points out that fireplaces of any kind are a rarity and luxury in south Florida and of course "unheard of by the Chamber of Commerce." He makes the most of this asset. He surrounds the opening of the fireplace with highly polished miter-edged black marble to contrast with the flat white wall. On both sides of the fireplace, he arranges furniture to face it.

For personal privacy, parts of the apartment are kept separate

The master bedroom suite, complete with its own bath and huge walk-in closet, can be closed to the rest of the world. So can the guest suite. A small dining ter-race by the kitchen is an intimate place for breaking bread. The apartment balances places of privacy with places for parties.

Materials are chosen for easy maintenance; colors, for a light look

If Florida is known first for its sunshine, Paterson wanted to reflect it all. He chose white for the walls and floors. The white tiles on the floor are not only reflective in color, they have a shiny surface of their own (easy to wetwash). The continuous white walls and floor also serve to unify the L-shaped space. Notice too that the floor tiles are placed on the diagonal—another device used to stretch the space.

The secondary color is green, the color of the upholstery. Green on white gives a cool, lush look, reminiscent of the tropical foliage of Florida. Made of canvas or cotton, upholstery materials are durable.

Light white coffee tables are of lacquered linen or Formica—both outstandingly long-lasting materials. Straw-colored end tables are of hardy Madagascar cloth. Both to set it off, and to echo the fireplace, the bar is sheathed in black Formica. Other accents in the entertaining area are pink. Appropriate. After all, who wouldn't be in the pink on a winter weekend here?

Sources

Floor tiles: FLORIDA TILES. Vertical louvers: HOLLAND SHADE CO. Custom upholstered furniture: THOMAS DeANGELIS, INC. Emerald green upholstery canvas and white pillow fabric: KENT-BRAGALINE. Green and white upholstery print: d.d. and LESLIE TILLETT, INC. Pink fabrics and white braid trim: BRUNSCHWIG & FILS. Black and white pillow fabric: MARGOWEN, INC. Coffee table in lacquered linen, end tables in Madagascar cloth: KARL SPRINGER LTD. Parsons table: BIELECKY BROS. INC. Wall lamps: HANSEN LAMPS. Lamp shades: WARD AND ROME. Canister lamp: LIGHTING ASSOCIATES. Bar-cabinet and Formica coffee table: custom designed by DONALD M. PATERSON. Andirons: EDWIN JACKSON, INC.

Photography by Ernest Silva

SUMMER HOUSE FOR
THREE GENERATIONS OF ONE FAMILY

Everybody's hot and tired of their work-a-day world. They want to cool off, relax, have fun. It's the summer season, and they want to get away from it all—but they want the family to be together. It's important for the grandparents, parents, and children to share the time of their lives. (It's also very important for them to be able to get away from one another every once in a while.)

This lucky family repairs to the Italian Riviera to a modern house designed by architects A. Savati and A. Tresoldi. Though we're unlikely to be invited to join them, we can get some ideas from their house. It has been designed to stimulate summer fun, to keep temperatures cool, to minimize maintenance, and to encourage all-family activities, as well as personal privacy. This house succeeds at simplifying life.

Stone floors, white walls, and minimal furnishings keep the house cool

Cardoso stone, a local material that resembles rough-cut marble, is cut in random shapes and used for all floors, both indoors and out. This hard, smooth material is cool under the toes.

All walls throughout the house are white, which gives the house a refreshing feeling.

Furnishings are kept down to their functional minimum. Uncluttered spaces are cooler than others. The furnishings themselves are the simplest possible shapes. In the hall there is a half-circle table attached to the wall, accompanied by two Z-chairs. In the dining room (page 98) a simple rectangular table has more Z-chairs around it, and the server is a simple semicircular shelf. Notice also that the billiard table in the living room and the piano in the music room are painted white to match the walls. This way they visually fade into the background and don't seem to crowd the cool, open space.

Notice that textures are mostly hard. The soft ones are smooth. No nubby surfaces to make you feel hot and sticky.

Bright colors and bold patterns create a fun-loving, stimulating effect

Against the cool neutral background of gray stone floors and white walls, bursts of color excite the space. All doors are lacquered red. All the sofas are upholstered in bold diagonal stripes. This exuberance suggests an "Ah, what the hell!" attitude. Why not let your hair down and have fun? This is not the place for tightly controlled constraint. This is a place to relax and let your creative juices flow. Bright colors and bold patterns give the go-go.

Wet-washable materials and simplicity keep cleaning to a minimum

It doesn't matter what you spill on the stone floors. Doors and closets are lacquered, so fingerprints wipe off with a wet cloth. Table tops are lacquered or laminated or covered with oil cloth. Chairs are simple (undust-catching) wooden shapes or upholstered with washable cloth. The two small boys can't get into too much trouble in this house, and no one has to spend vacation time preoccupied with cleaning. (Who would want to anyway?)

The entryway is sculptured in a semicircular shape. The living room and music room are to the left, the kitchen and dining room to the right. The elevator serves three floors. Upper floors contain bedrooms, baths, and a roof garden for dining.

Photography by Laura Salvati

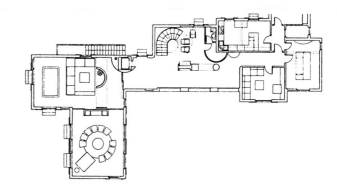

Dining indoors is kept simple. Furnishings are a rectangular table, Z-chairs, and a serving shelf manufactured by ATELIER INTERNATIONAL *under license from* CASSINA. *Lamps:* STILNOVO.

Sliding doors allow areas to open for sociability or close for privacy

There are times when the boys want to play by themselves, the parents want to pursue their hobbies in peace, and the grandparents want to retreat from it all. With many of the rooms designed with sliding doors, each generation can find solitary solace. A person can close off his or her private place. Sliding doors are a wonderfully simple solution to our changing needs for people and privacy.

How have the architects succeeded in simplifying life?

Most of us feel we go through contortions getting the job done, pleasing the family, being responsible in the community, and finally trying to be true to ourselves. Does life need to be so complicated? Is it as the Chinese think—a simple balance between yin and yang—an organization of opposites? It is in this home! Cool colors are balanced with warm ones. Hard textures are balanced with soft ones. Straight shapes are balanced with rounded ones. To achieve an essential harmony, the architects have balanced opposites.

Sofas with cool stripes are adorned with warm-colored pillows. Deep green stripes on the living room sofas are complemented by pillows in golden hues. Blue stripes on the sofas in

The living room, to the left of the entry, features sunken seating facing a fireplace. In back of the seating, out of the pit, is a big billiard table. Through a sliding door is the music room, where auditorium seating has been bolted to the stone floor in a circle around the piano.

the upstairs sitting room are complemented by pink pillows. In a small sitting niche, there's the opposite effect: warm red stripes on the sofa are complemented by cool blue pillows.

Soft upholstery throughout the home provides a balance to hard-surfaced floors, walls, and tables. Note particularly the loose, soft shape of the green canvas chair in the front hallway and in the upstairs sitting room.

Throughout the home, straight shapes are balanced with rounded ones. The rounded front hall leads off into square and rectangular rooms. The Z-chairs and the diamond-shaped mirror in the front hall are balanced by a rounded shelf and a rounded planter. The mostly straight shapes in the living room are balanced by the mostly rounded shapes in the adjacent music room. The best example of all is an upstairs bedroom. There's a dynamic checkerboard grid on the bedspread, the closet doors, and the desk table top. These forceful straight shapes are balanced by the rounded bed frame and the rounded arm chair. The house is a harmony of essential elements.

Warm and cool balance in two seating areas. In a small niche, a red striped sofa is accented with blue pillows. In an upstairs sitting room, a blue striped sofa is accented with pink pillows. In the kitchen, adjacent to the dining room, slick black cabinets contrast with wood and wicker stools.

A dramatic upstairs bedroom contrasts squared shapes with circular. A large green and white checkerboard patterns the bedspread, the floor-to-ceiling closet doors, and the desk top. The hard lacquered surfaces have been perfectly matched to the soft cloth.

PART FOUR:

SENSE OF SELF IN SPACE AND TIME

Why do so many of us love to travel to Europe? Isn't it a thrill to realize that Napoleon or Caesar may have stood on the same spot of earth that's under your feet? Isn't it wonderful to imagine the panoply of the past? Frankly, I can't walk down the grand staircase of any old castle without fantasizing that I'm a princess in a rustling long silk gown. But for a few generations (and certainly some changes in circumstances), that could have been my life!

Part of the thrill of travel, I think, is to realize the humanness of our heroes. A tourist attraction in Corinth, Greece, is the ancient latrine. People had to pay to get in, and God forbid if you were a traveler and didn't have the coin of the realm! With seats lined up like those in the theater, the latrine seems to have been an unpretentious place for a casual chat. Here, in Greece, in the same country that gave us the seeds of our civilization, the purity of the Parthenon, the world's most marvelous marble sculptures, is an acknowledgment that the human condition remains the same. We have a lot in common with the people of the past. Our everyday needs are much the same. Our potential, like theirs, is anything we can imagine and support. To realize their humanness helps us accept ours with less embarrassment. To realize their transcendence is to realize that we *can* reclaim our dreams. And the weight of the world isn't all on our shoulders. We don't have to reinvent the wheel. We can profit from the past and build on it. (The plumbing and air-circulation system in that latrine *were* well engineered!)

A sense of the past enriches the present

Not only do we have an information base to build on, so that we, with our creativity, can push forward the frontiers of learning, we have something softer. Acceptance. Self-esteem. We, like those before us, belong in the continuity of time. We have our own cultural context. We matter. Architect Robert A. M. Stern explains his view of the importance of the past: "When our clients don't articulate their affections for the past, we search these out. Not because the past is better than the present, but because the past represents the touchstone of cultural continuity. And when you have cultural continuity, you have meaning."

We have been living uprooted—without a past

Roots are nurturing, as any plant would tell you. However, through the years many of us have been living abstracted from our past. The design elite had had it with posts and lintels, with ruffles and chintzes. The classic, the traditional, the cluttered and cozy were all out. The Modern Movement that started at the beginning of this century wanted to toss out tradition and create a new social and visual order based on the efficiencies of the machine. Technology was the turn-on. It could lead the way out of the morass of two world wars, away from emotional excess, to a clean pure human state. Nice idea. However, it couldn't endure. It was inhuman.

People got tired of hard-edged anonymous spaces where their human needs for individuality, sensuality, sentimentality were rigorously uprooted and denied. A Modernist housing project in St. Louis is a classic case. The architectural pundits admired it; gave it a design award. However, the people who had to live in it vandalized it so often that it finally had to be dynamited out of existence!

The human spirit will not be denied. It's nice to watch how the human spirit seeks balance. When the Modern Movement began, it sought purity and simplicity in reaction to the excessive ornamentation of the Victorian era. Now after living with excessive purity and simplicity for over half a century, we're ready for some clutter, confusion—illusion. We want to reclaim the pleasures of our past. We don't want to feel like transients in time, living in clean machines that won't show a trace of our humanity. We want to belong to the place where we live and to the continuum of time.

Where do you live? How can you sink your roots in its soil?

How can you sense that your home is your own, but that you and your home are an important part of the community? How can you link what you are with where you are?

What's important to you in terms of your living needs? What inspires you about the past and the present of the place where you live? How can you coordinate your needs with a respect for some of the traditions of the place? We show some different solutions—all expressive of individuality.

A young couple, comfortable with cozy small spaces, chose to restore an historic landmark house in Nantucket. An older couple, preferring airy openness and minimal maintenance, built a new house in Nantucket with large rooms and lots of space. The style of the house, however, reflects the traditions of Nantucket. There's even a widow's walk on the roof (even though it's highly unlikely that the retired husband will be lost at sea). The owners of a ski lodge tucked under the magnificent mountains of the American West built a third floor onto their lodge so that they could enjoy an unobstructed view of the inspiring sunsets from the warmth of the indoors. New residents of Miami appreciated a view too. They wanted an unobstructed view of Biscayne Bay, and they wanted their own private pool where they could swim laps. Instead of opting for a conventional home with the pool in the back, these people selected an architect who built them an individualized home. Stretching out along the shore, measuring an unusual 110 x 27 feet (33 x 8 meters), the home enjoys a fabulous wide-open view of Biscayne Bay. The pool, in front of the house, is also an unconventionally long size [60 x 10 feet (18 x 3 meters)]. To harmonize this strange structure with the traditions of Miami, the architects chose conventional building materials—concrete blocks, cement, and stucco—materials that have a long history of weathering the Miami climate. They also linked the home with the past by coloring it pink, a hue long associated with Florida and the Caribbean.

Your home can reflect the traditions of the place where you live in all sorts of ways. It can be actually old, made to look old; it can be designed to harmonize with the landscape; its colors and materials can be traditional, while its shape and structure are unique. There are all sorts of creative ways to blend your needs and wishes for accommodation with the heritage of the region.

Your interior furnishings also can make reference to the local traditions that appeal to you. The young couple in the Nantucket historic house love to collect old artifacts. Their home is filled with folk art, antiques, island furniture, and scrimshaw of Nantucket's whaling days. The older couple in Nantucket prefer contemporary furnishings, but they make references to the island's past with selected accessories. A Chinese bowl, suggestive of Nantucket's past tea trade with the Far East, is filled with native Nantucket flowers. A Chinese altar cloth ornaments the wall of the foyer. The ski lodge in the West brings the atmosphere of the great outdoors inside with rustic log furniture. The Indian influence is attested to by tribal drums, bought at a local market and used as coffee tables in the family room. In the Miami house, furnishings are colored pink, Florida's heritage hue.

You can pick from the local history whatever objects or ideas appeal to you, and you can use them in your own individualized way. By doing so you are harmonizing your lifestyle with the heritage of the place. You are placing your roots in the native soil and nurturing your own growth.

Would you like more romance and excitement in your life?

You can give your life dimension and a sense of excitement by incorporating references to the past in your everyday life. What period of history excites you? Swashbuckling pirates? The romance under the stiff social surface of Victorian England? Do you enjoy historic novels? Or the plays on public television? Who are your heroes? Heroines? Why not give yourself a little mysterious allure by suggesting your favorite era in your own home. It will make people wonder—and with wonder comes fascination. Invest in your own fascination. After all, there are many levels to your personality. After satisfying your practical needs, it's important to feed your spirit—maybe it's even *more* important than satisfying your practical needs.

Charles Addams, the macabre cartoonist, has decked out his mobile van as a somewhat ghoulish Victorian parlor, complete with stuffed birds and stained glass. He feels right at home on the road. A young person coming to Manhattan with dreams of glamour and glory could feel depressed if the grim reality of a one-room flat and a next-to-nothing budget closed in on him. Yet grim reality need not be a suffocating shell. This person broke out of it. He gave his humble flat the illusion of glamour and glory by decorating it in Art Deco, the sparkling style of the 30s. Illusion can cast out the demons, deny depression—even inexpensively.

What period of the past best expresses the feelings you'd like to feel?

Try to identify the feelings you'd like to feel in your home. Then rifle through books and magazines and find a period of the past that best expresses the look you'd like. You can design your home to inspire in you the feelings you'd like to feel. Do you like earthy elegance? Maybe Tudor is for you. Do you like a cozy sense of romance? Maybe you'll go for little Victorian prints and ruffles. Do you like elegant formality? Maybe 18th-century English is your style. Do you like to project power? Maybe you'll go for Napoleon's Empire style.

You can suggest a style without spending fortunes looking for period antiques and artifacts. What colors were characteristic of the style you like? What textures? Rough or smooth? Hard or soft? What shapes seemed typical? Rounded forms or square or rectangular ones or something else altogether? By playing with the characteristic colors, textures, and shapes, you can suggest a style, have all its evocative effect, with relatively little expense. You don't even have to darken the door of an antique store.

Suggesting dimensions in time is a new trend with architects and designers

There's contentment in continuity. Feeling a spiritual alliance with the peoples of the past makes us feel less alone, isolated. The glass and steel grids, the hard-edged furnishings of the Modern Movement, and its emphasis on abstraction eventually made us feel out of the running in the human race. The International Style denied sensuality and spirituality in favor of order and intellectualism. Now even many architects are tired of it. They too want softness, sentiment, serendipity.

Wonderful things are being dug up from the trashed past. Ornaments from architecture, found in junk yards, have become wall art, bases for cocktail tables, stands for sculpture. Classical columns where they exist in architecture are coming out of hiding. The concealing modern facades or built-around boxes are being peeled away. Columns are being used as less serious support structures than ever before. We show one supporting a toaster. Architects and designers are using architectural elements of the past in a whimsical way. They are showing their consciousness of continuity with good humor. They are not burdening us with academic earnestness. Columns, pediments, moldings—all are being used decoratively to enchant the eye, to cast shadows and illusions of depth. Walls look less flat and confining. These old architectural elements give a sense of depth to space, and they give us a sense of depth in time. In some ways, the past takes the pressure off the present, and isn't that a pleasant way to live?

RELATING TO THE HERITAGE OF THE REGION

NANTUCKET:
18th-CENTURY SHIPPING CENTER

The new, built to look old.

Photography by Harry Hartman

The foyer of the new house features a slate floor, Oriental rugs, a Hepplewhite settee, and a Chinese altar cloth. A glimpse of the living room with MCGUIRE chairs, a Burmese head, book-lined wall reveals a simple eclecticism.

The heritage of Nantucket Island excites the imagination and stirs the soul. In the 18th century, Nantucket was an important center of the whaling industry and port for the adventurous sea captains who sailed to the Far East to purchase the rich treasures of that exotic culture. The wealth of the world was sought at sea and brought home to Nantucket. Adventure and endurance, wealth and wonder mesh in the rich fabric of the island's past. Those living in Nantucket today become part of the island's time continuum. The island's rich past enriches their present days.

Linking your present with the past of the place where you live is one wonderful way to feel rooted, to feel that you belong. In Nantucket, it can't really be otherwise. The exteriors of all houses in Nantucket must conform to standards prescribed by the Historic District Commission. On these pages you can compare a new house, built to look old, with an old house, restored to look new. In both, you have the best of both worlds: modern convenience and cleanliness, as well as a sense of the past in the present.

The modern house (on the left) was built in 1970 according to Nantucket traditions. (Notice the widow's walk on the roof.) The house on the right is an authentic Nantucket landmark house. Its clapboard front and shingled sides are typical of the oldest houses that hug the island's streets.

Interestingly, a young couple restored the old house and an older couple retired to the new house. Both couples interpret Nantucket's traditions in ways that best reflect their own interests.

A contemporary recollection of the past

Although true to tradition in its outward appearance, the new house is much larger, with bigger rooms, than those of the island's past. Designed by Boston architect Philip Gray and decorated with the help of the Hendriks brothers of Nantucket, the home evokes a contemporary recollection of the past. Generally furnished with contemporary styles, the home makes reference to the island's English heritage and to its trade with the Orient. The foyer is furnished with an 18th-century English-style Hepplewhite settee and a Chinese altar cloth. The sofa in the living room is set on a Chinese-style base. A Chinese bowl is filled with native Nantucket flowers. There is a comforting coherence of past and present.

A landmark house, full of traditional treasures

The landmark house, lovingly restored and furnished by its owners, decorator Diane Chase Madden and her antique-loving husband, reflects the couple's interest in collecting objects of the island's past. Folk art, antiques, island furniture, and even scrimshaw—all find nooks to nestle in, in this cozy, comfortable house. The island's whaling days are suggested not only by scrimshaw, but by whale-oil lamps and a Liverpool jug named after the famous whaling captain Thomas Starbuck. The inhabitants' English origins are suggested by a collection of 18th-century English candlesticks in the sitting room, English export ceramics in the dining room, a spider-leg tea table, and a Chippendale chair in the front parlor. Canton ware and Oriental rugs are among the things that reflect

The old, restored to look new.

The front hall and "Captain's Corner" set the mood for the old house where every corner and surface is highlighted by period pieces indigenous to Nantucket—like an early 19th-century clock, a hanging corner shelf with baskets and a Liverpool jug, "Thomas Starbuck," circa 1800.

the riches first brought to the island by staunch sea captains. Despite the extent of the collections and the small size of the house, the home seems welcoming not only to additional treasures but to the daily life of the couple and their active teenage son.

With an active sense of the past, the present often has more meaning

Feeling linked with the past, particularly with one so laced with adventure and achievement, gives one an enhanced sense of self. One is aware of one's part in the larger picture—in the continuity of time.

In the new house, the living room is furnished with an airy arrangement of simple shapes (easy to maintain). Bright greens excite the space, and Oriental accessories allude to Nantucket's traditional trade with the Far East. Rattan chairs: MCGUIRE. *Rug:* V'SOSKE. *Barrel chair:* BAKER KNAPP & TUBBS. *Drapery and trim:* SCALAMANDRE. *Pair of paintings:* VIRGINIA GREENLEAF KOCH.

The front parlor of the restored house has been furnished with the type of antiques that a wealthy sea captain would have collected during his journeys around the world. The owners found many of these treasures on the island. The window treatment is a mid-18th-century French design. The spider-leg tea table is 18th-century English; the secretary is French Directoire. Other distinguished objects include a 19th-century Napoleonic bronze doré clock.

(Left) Originally intended as a dining room, this area has evolved into a family room. The walls and ceiling are lacquered black/green. The floor is dark green Vermont marble. Simple sofas, a YALE R. BURGE table, a sisal area rug are highlighted by a stained glass window framed by brass LEVOLOR blinds.

(Above) A delightful vignette in the contemporary Nantucket house reflects the living room with its pared-down elegance. The contemporary Chinese bowl is filled with native flowers: Queen Anne's lace and bachelor buttons. The mirror with bevelled glass is framed in American Victorian molded copper.

(Left) Today's dining room, originally the keeping room, documents the influence of the China trade on Nantucket with Canton ware and American pewter whale oil lamps. A late-18th-century Pennsylvania corner cupboard with its original finish is filled with Nantucket silver and English export ceramics.

(Above) Flaming candles in a collection of 18th-century English candlesticks warm the cozy sitting room of the traditional house. Over the mantle are a pair of 17th-century Dutch landscapes and a pair of 18th-century Dutch vases. All the rare antiques in this room serve the same purpose for which they were designed.

A SKI LODGE IN THE GOLDEN WEST

Snow-capped mountains are inspiring. What a glorious grandeur of space! The air is crisp and cold and scented with the smell of the pines that climb the mountains. The sunshine is golden rich. Still wild and wonderful, this place in the past belonged only to Nature and the Indians.

William Gaylord, a member of the American Society of Interior Designers, was asked to design the interior of a ski lodge at the base of these majestic mountains. From his office in San Francisco, Gaylord designs for clients around the world. When given this commission, he had recently completed a beach house in Hawaii, an apartment in New York, and an embassy in Washington. A man of great taste and sophistication, Gaylord knows many secrets to successful design.

He related the design of the lodge to the heritage of the region

He brought the beauty of nature indoors. To provide additional space for sleeping and to allow for the *indoor* enjoyment of the magnificent Western sunsets, Gaylord added a third-level loft to the two-story lodge. It is in this lounging area where early evening parties gather to enjoy the end of the day before descending the stairs to group around the fireplace below.

Echoing the woodlands outdoors and the golden wood tones of the architectural detailing, Gaylord chose wooden furniture in the same golden tones. To stand up to the size of the space, outdoors and in, the wood furniture is large in scale. Tall bookcases on either side of the fireplace emphasize the height of the two-story space. Massive log furniture in a bedroom and the family room enhance the rusticity of the environment.

To contrast with the cold outdoors, Gaylord designed the lodge to feel warm and welcoming. Rich neutral textures create an air of cozy comfort. Lights within the wooden bookshelves echo the glow of the fire. In a bedroom, a canopy bed, warmed with a down cover, is a toasty retreat. Tapestry wall hangings in the dining room and family room warm the walls.

To create a pure air, all materials are natural. Fabrics are of real fibers or skins. The living room coffee table and a number of other tables are marble. Natural tapestry weavings, hand-woven baskets, and fresh (some flowering) plants ornament the space.

Best of all, Indian tribal drums, found in a local market, are used as coffee tables in the family room. Through this gesture, Gaylord acknowledges the influence of the Indians in the heritage of the area and harmonizes not only the home, but the present with the past.

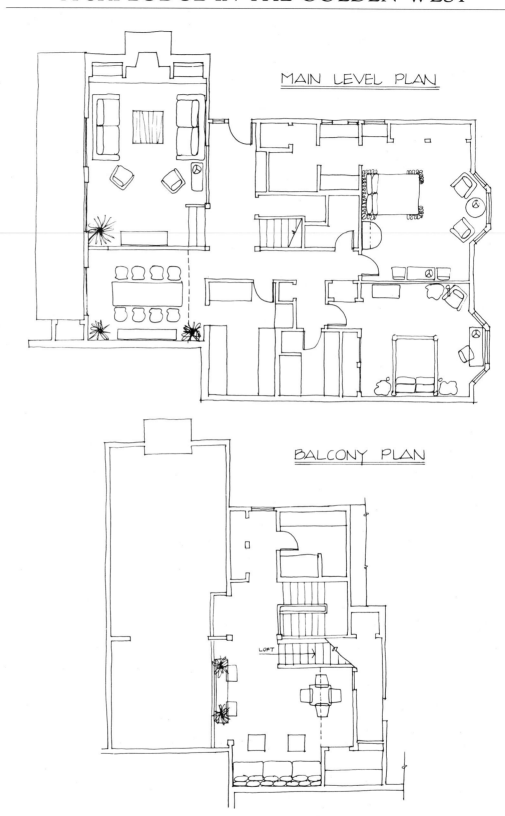

MAIN LEVEL PLAN

BALCONY PLAN

LOFT

The height of the living room—two stories—is emphasized by the bookcases at each end of the fireplace. The warm lights of the glowing fire are restated by lamps hidden behind the shelves.

(Top) Log bed and tables (LON-DON-MARQUIS) serve as the focal point of this bedroom. The Parsons bench at the window is covered in calf's skin. The bedcover and pillow cases are an unlined plise fabric (JACK LENOR LARSEN) that can be machine washed. The pillow cases come off for cleaning simply by untying the corners. The basket over the bed is a baby's cradle from the Philippines.

(Bottom) A cozy canopy bed is warmed by a down cover. The STROHEIM & ROMANN crewel fabric is used to upholster all visible parts of the bed, including the headboard.

A long trestle table, surrounded by captain's chairs, provides a setting for informal dining. The natural

(Top) A banquette has been designed for the wall of the family room. Clad in BRUNSCHWIG & FILS fabric, it is deep enough to function as a bed for sleep-in guests. Indian tribal drums, found locally, serve as coffee tables. Log furniture: LONDON-MARQUIS. Tapestry by Carolyn Cates.

(Bottom) The loft is used for early evening entertaining. Later it converts into a bedroom as the banquette opens to a queen-size bed. Fabric: BRUNSCHWIG & FILS.

environment is accented by a blue Robert Motherwell tapestry, flanked by two large plants.

LOCAL COLOR IN MIAMI

The house is unconventional for sure. It is nothing like its beige and brown split-level neighbors. In the exclusive bedroom community of Miami Shores, this strange structure may have caused the neighbors to fear for the cohesiveness of their community. But the architects knew: "Conventional" isn't the only way to tie in with the character of the community.

The architects used colors long associated with Florida and the Caribbean

Don't you think of Florida when you see a pink flamingo? The architectural firm of Arquitectonica chose pink flamingo colors and then graded them in different tones to define different areas of the home. The front steps, placed along the side of the house, are deep maroon. The front facade wall (concealing the pool) is red, and the major exterior walls of the home are pale pink. The colors come inside too. The comfortable lounge chairs in the library are also pink, Florida's heritage hue.

Although the shape of the structure is unconventional [110 x 27 feet (33 x 8 meters)], the building materials aren't. The architects chose materials with a happy history of withstanding the climate: concrete blocks, cement, and a little stucco. Sensible can be stylish.

Innovations take advantage of the site and serve the clients' preferences.

Do you want to be stuck with conventions when they don't serve you? No? Well, neither did these clients. Although all the houses in the neigborhood had their pools in the back, architect Hervin Romney saw the value of putting the pool in front so that the house would have an unobstructed view of Biscayne Bay in the back. Then for privacy at the pool, he built the front facade wall. The glass bricks in the facade admit light while promoting privacy. A curious passerby may only peer into the pool by peeking through the porthole in front.

The pool itself is unconventional also. Long and narrow—60 x 10 feet (18 x 3 meters)—it is specifically designed for the clients who like to swim laps rather than just splash around. As these architects have indicated, it is possible to serve your own needs and find a unique way to unify your home with the heritage of its location.

Sources

Sofa and chairs: INTERIOR DESIGNERS (Miami). Patio furniture: BROWN JORDAN.

LINKING THE PRESENT WITH THE PAST

MAKING CONNECTIONS: THE POSTMODERN MOVEMENT

We've been feeling uprooted, disconnected. Much of the world around us has seemed cold, austere, unsympathetic to our human needs. Designers wanted us to part with our favorite old chairs, couldn't tolerate our figurines. Everything had to be disciplined, clean, organized. We were instructed to clean out our closets and our lives, to free ourselves from the burden of memories. We were told it was going to be a brave new world. Machine technology was going to show us a better way to live. This was the philosophy of the Modern Movement.

Beginning in the first years of this century, the Modern Movement reacted to the eclectic excesses of the Victorian period and to its poorly made machine adaptations of traditional styles. Architects and designers wanted to make a clean start. They wanted to use the technology of the machine to create a new order of design. They wanted to create objects that *looked* machine made. They wanted to purify and simplify—to bring a rational mathematical order to human life.

Time has passed. We no longer feel satiated or suffocated by the clutter of Victorian parlors (actually, I think we find them rather charming). We have been living a long time with cold glass and steel skyscrapers and minimal machinemades. We feel starved for some softness, some sentiment, some surprise. We want *human values* to replace those of the machine. We know, from our own lack of satisfaction, that efficiency isn't the only condition of human happiness.

Now old is new

Today architects and designers are on to us. Being creative, they want something new too. Now old is new. We no longer have to hide our heritage as if it were a lunatic relative best kept in the attic. Architects who a few years ago would build geometric boxes to hide old structural supports are now happy to expose the pillars of the past. Columns are *in*. Allusions to old architectural orders are *in*. Any sort of suggestion that today's humanity is part of the continuum of the human race is now *okay*. Thank God.

Do you remember how strongly Alex Haley's book *Roots* touched the public? Alex Haley understood. He explained, "The universal appeal of *Roots* is based on the average American's longing for a sense of heritage." A lot of us were inspired to try to trace our own heritages, to try to get a sense of our own roots. Even if we never could locate a family Bible with old entries, we became respectful of our own histories. We recognized that we are the seed of the people before us. We can share pride in their achievements, compassion for their problems, and amusement at their foibles. Acknowledging their humanity allows us to acknowledge ourselves.

Interpreting tradition in inventive ways

Recognizing the human need for connection and continuity, architects and designers are today, as we've said, making references to the past. But they are not buying it wholesale. They are not rebuilding Versailles or Williamsburg. They are interpreting traditional motifs in their own inventive ways. They are acknowledging the past, not duplicating it. They want to make their own statement in their own time.

Where old architectural elements exist, they are showing them off. In Michael Schwarting's loft (opposite), the original structural column—a fine fluted one with a Corinthian capital—is exposed. It stands in dramatic contrast to the smooth modern multifunctional living structure. The total interior is one that bespeaks today. It acknowledges the past, but is living in the present. In the kitchen/living/

dining area pictured on the middle of page 115, owner architect Turner Brooks has a supportive column in the center of the space. It and old artifacts symbolize a cozy continuity in time.

Sometimes architects treat traditional motifs in a whimsical way. For his East Hampton, Long Island, house (page 115 right), architect Robert A. M. Stern made cut-out columns and a pediment in silhouette to frame his front door.

In the New Haven home shown on the near right, Ben Benedict and Carl Pucci of Bumpzoid Architects use a truncated column to support a toaster. As you can see, contemporary architects are giving new interpretations to the classic column support system. This one has no structural function at all. It does, however, hold up the toaster. It also has a visual design function. It is one in a series of columns aligned to draw the eye down the length of the room, making the room seem larger.

Stern, a leader of the Postmodern Movement, often uses columns decoratively. In his conversion of an old Park Avenue apartment (opposite), he creates a kind of cut-out wall. Something surprising to help us out of the totally predictable mathematical order of the Modern Movement. Notice the variety of shapes above the columns. Why? Who knows? Stern likes to keep us guessing. Feels we need a little mystery in our lives.

Putting you in the picture

"For so long we've had so few subjects for design, mostly they were machine processes, mostly they were about how to make anything as minimal as possible," states Stern. "I say the world's much more interesting than that!" Instead of stressing the simplest, most abstract, most generalized solution like the Modernists before him, Stern "rejects the prototypical solution in favor of the individual case." Something unique and personal, suited to the client and the space. Something surprising. Something suggestive of another era. Something decorative to delight the eye. "I think there is a human inclination to ornament oneself and one's surroundings. I am in reaction to the absence of orna-

mentation in architecture...." Stern feels that Modernism represented the architects' values while Postmodernism represents *society's* values.

"The Modernism of the 20s and 30s left us with an architecture that made no references to the past and also made very few, if any, references to human size, to the human condition. It was, therefore, truly abstract. That's why I'm in reaction to it.

"Traditional architectural elements ... help you to relate to the room, put you in the picture. You can imagine your height in relationship to it."

In a renovation of a 1906 carriage house on Long Island (see next page), Stern gives further expression to his philosophy. Classical columns are used decoratively throughout the house. Moldings are used inventively to add interest—dimension, shadows, historical allusions—to the walls. Custom cabinetry is designed in shapes suggestive of ancient Greece and Rome. To illustrate by another example, in the master bedroom of a 1950s vacation house (page 119), Stern has designed what he calls "a temple of love." The bed's headboard consists of a triumphal arch and a Palladian motif resting on a keystone shape. This certainly is the place in which to worship your own personal Greek god or goddess!

The stairway of the Long Island carriage house features the contrast of sleek free-standing brass handrails with delicate moldings outlining the shape of the stairs. Suggestions of the past in the present.

Stern further explains his affection for traditional motifs: "When our clients don't articulate their affections for the past, we search these out. Not because the past is better than the present, but because the past represents the touchstone of cultural continuity. And when you have cultural continuity, you have meaning."

The Modernist credo was "Less is more." Architect Robert Venturi answers: "Less is a bore." Postmodern spokesman Stern retorts: "More is more."

Sources

Upholstered armchairs: SAPORITI ITALIA.

Photography by Robert Perron

The renovation of a 1906 Long Island carriage house by architect Robert A. M. Stern is designed with the classical architectural elements of columns and moldings to give visual dimension to the space and spiritual dimension to its place in time. The moldings around the window panes and the moldings on the walls catch the light to create intriguing shadow patterns.

(Top) Stern's "temple of love" in the master bedroom of a 1950s vacation house. To create his unique headboard, Stern explored the grand shapes of classical architecture in a smaller scale. His composition consists of a miniaturized triumphal arch, Palladian motifs, and the classic keystone.

(Below) The stairway of the Long Island carriage house shows Stern's desire to design an undateable house. The sleek handrails suggest something modern. The delicate moldings suggest something traditional.

Photography by Robert Per

In a tiny one-room New York apartment, with a budget a little less than $3,000, designer Robert Shaw was able to create a sense of glamour and grandeur.

Shaw suggested Art Deco with textures, colors, and shapes rather than with expensive objects

Instead of buying precious pieces from the period, Shaw evoked the Art Deco ambience by choosing its characteristic smooth textures—mirror, tile, velvet—its characteristic colors—sophisticated grays, blacks, tans, and peaches—and its characteristic shapes—the ziggurat and the circle.

Because the apartment did have the blessing of a fireplace, Shaw wanted to emphasize it dramatically. By a stroke of luck, the designer found an actual inexpensive Art Deco relic in an old hotel—a piece of peach-colored mirror. He carefully cut it into two semicircles to frame the sides of the fireplace. In the center section above, he filled in with a rounded panel of ordinary mirror.

Facing the fireplace, Shaw positioned a sleeping/sitting unit, covered in smooth gray to match the carpet. To give the sofa/bed back-up support, Shaw built a storage unit behind it. The storage unit faces the front door, creating an entry while providing privacy to the seating area. The bolsters in the back of the bed are squared shapes that build up to a ziggurat shape. They echo the shape of the coffee table in front.

To give architectural interest to the room and to prevent the eye from wandering to the ceiling with its clutter of pipes and beams, Shaw painted the walls in two tones of tan—not quite up to the ceiling—and separated the shades with an eye-catching orange and white stripe at chair-rail level.

At the windows, Shaw repeated the room's horizontal lines with an inexpensive structure of wooden slats over roller shades. Two casual chairs complete the scheme. The luxurious look of this apartment was created with more ingenuity than expense. When company's coming, the client borrows actual Art Deco andirons from a friend.

PART FIVE:

EXPRESSING INDIVIDUALITY

How do you make your home your own? How do you make it a personalized place? I'm reminded of a business woman who traveled more than she would have liked. She felt desperate in the anonymous spaces of hotel rooms, separated from her family, friends, and familiar objects. But she did find a way to ease the pain. On every business trip, she packed up small framed portraits of her favorite folks, plus lengths of her favorite fabrics. When she reached yet another heartless hotel room, she would cover the bureau top with a familiar fabric, drape the chair, tie a snazzy scarf around a lampshade or a pillow, and put out the portraits of the people who warmed her life. She made the hotel room home. She personalized the place.

Moving can be traumatizing too. The new place seems cold and impersonal until you make it your own. And how dreary and dismal it is to sit in an empty, echoing room, waiting for the furniture to be delivered. (It's a good idea to go out and buy a bunch of flowers to soothe your spirits.) Even when the new home is a vast improvement over the old, its unfamiliarity is off-putting. After moving out of my fourth-floor walk-up, I cried myself to sleep for the first three nights in my fancy new highrise. The walls were blank; the space was empty. I could have been anybody.

It's not a comfortable feeling to believe you could be anybody. It's better to be in an environment that supports your uniqueness, that builds on and enhances your interests, cherishes your happy memories, and comforts you when you're down.

How can you individualize your interior?

Surround yourself with favorite objects. What means something to you? Your tennis trophies? Pictures picked up in your travels? Your African spears? Your Victorian valentines? An antique chair from your grandmother? Your favorite objects will express your interests and personalize your place.

Do you have a collection of any kind?

Antiques? Pottery? Porcelain? Rugs? Books? Old snow shoes? Even in the most anonymous of architectural spaces, your collection can express your individuality. Designer Andrew Tauber houses an exquisite collection of Louis XVI gilt bronze and Chinese Ch'ien and K'ang Hsi furniture, paintings and porcelain—all in an ordinary New York apartment. He thinks the apartment is a good neutral background for his fine furnishings. Inspired by his Chinese screen, he painted the walls green. A young couple, complete with small child, gave their neutral New Jersey summer home individuality and élan by spreading around their wealth of wonderful kilim carpets.

Your collection can inspire your entire design scheme

Why not make the most of your assets? If you have a special collection, why not emphasize it? How? If your something special is in the background—on the walls and/or the floor—you can emphasize it by underplaying the foreground furnishings. You can make them neutral or blend-into-the-background colors. If you have something special in the foreground—furniture and/or accessories—you can emphasize this attraction by underplaying the background walls and floor. Since you can't have everything in the room clamoring for your attention, it's best to emphasize your assets and underplay your liabilities.

You will see examples of a choice between emphasis on the background or the foreground in this chapter. The lady with the exciting wrap-around mural in her bedroom chose to cover her furnishings in a color that would blend in with the walls. The couple with the wonderful rugs chose to color their furnishings in neutral wood and sand tones. The collector of books and handcrafted accessories chose to set them off with a bland background—white walls and a white rug.

People often derive their color schemes from their special objects. The couple who inherited an antique French chair from grandmother used its brown and beige coloring as a theme for a muted color scheme. The executive with a collection of blue and white porcelain set it off in a white wall system against a bright blue wall.

The color of your collection can give your design direction, but so can its size, shape, texture, and even age. Things of similar size go together. They seem to belong to the same family. Things of similar shape go together too. For example, one gentleman, striving for a look of seasoned elegance, decided he would buy nothing made after the late 1920s. His collection incorporates Art Nouveau and Art Deco objects, 18th-century Italian bronzes, a signed Louis XV armchair in its original fabric, and a pair of 1795 French chairs from the estate of

King Farouk. Elegant and expensive, n'est-ce pas? What makes it all go together? Most of the furnishings and objects are characterized by curves. Curved things go together.

Another reason that this gentleman's collection coordinates is that it is all similarly smooth and sleek. Fine refined textures work well together. Alternatively, rough and ready textures look right together. Gere Kavanaugh's collection of handcrafts is characterized by an earthy naturalness, a feeling she loves.

You might even discover, when you consider it, that the things you love may well be characterized by a certain sort of texture, shape, or size. When you've got these characteristics identified, not only will it be easier for you to find more favorite objects, but you can use these traits to characterize your whole home! Is what you like large or small? Straight or curved? Rough or smooth? Or something in between?

To design a home that portrays your personality, you might well be inspired by a favorite object or collection. As we have suggested, you might take the colors, size, shape, and texture of the object or collection and make them the dominant characteristics of your home. To add excitement and spark, you then need to do something contrary.

A contrast will give your interior excitement, energy

Too much of even a good thing is too much. A contrast will keep you from being bored by monotony. In an atmosphere of antiques a modern piece has pizzazz. The exquisite elegance of Andrew Tauber's antique French and Chinese pieces is emphasized by his inclusion of a modern lucite desk. Tauber explains, "I think you have to do one shot of something modern in this setting. That's why I bought the desk." Conversely, an old piece in a modern setting gives a room a sense of life. Isn't it dull when everybody agrees about everything? And everything is predictable? Oh, ho-hum. Surprises delight and excite.

How can you keep your collection in control?

Marjorie Helsel states the designer's dilemma: "I feel that as an interior designer, one is privileged to be privy to all cultures and most technologies. It seems inevitable that one becomes a collector and what you bring 'home' from this tremendous exposure is the silt of your reactions and selective eye: a traditional classic there, a contemporary classic here, some things reverent, some naive, some just amusing. However, unlike a client project which has a definite beginning and end, you could easily emerge in the progress of a career in a mountain of clutter." How does she keep it under control? Color coordination. She sets off her objects with neutral walls and floor. By color, she blends some furnishings into the background. She updates and emphasizes other furnishings with upholstery in stand-out contemporary colors. Her living room, as a result, "is almost a microcosm in the process of collecting. My first purchase, an 18th-century sofa, and my most recent, the provocative Chinese faces silk-screened on the sofa pillows, are both here." Careful color coordination makes it work.

Rather than underplay and color coordinate, Andrew Tauber has another answer to not being run out of house and home by accumulated collections. "I think collecting antiques becomes, well, like a disease for many people," he explains. "They fill up the house, then they add even more." Tauber has licked the problem. He has a rule. "I sell three or four pieces and use the money to buy one incredible piece. Friends are always saying: 'You buy more and more each year, but you seem to have less and less.' Now, that's collecting." In addition to having objects of finer quality, Tauber has more space in which to set them off.

Purchasing objects that appeal to you and having them around you is a way to enhance your environment and make it your own. These are concrete objects that you can see and touch. Another way to express yourself in your home is to get in touch with the images in your mind—your fantasies.

What fantasies do you have that give you good feelings?

If you could indentify your fantasies, write them down, there may be some wonderful way to give them the illusion of reality in your own home. Marjorie Borradaile Helsel loves parties. She dreamed of a constant festive fete, surrounded by her friends—all dressed up and looking swell, with a waiter entering with iced champagne and a perky maid arranging wondrous flowers. Wouldn't it be wonderful? It would indeed. If such an atmosphere makes Helsel feel delicious delight, why not create the atmosphere to elicit the mood? She did. She hired a painter to create a wrap-around mural on the walls of her bedroom. He invented the perfect party—one that never has to end. Helsel sleeps and wakes up surrounded by an atmosphere that elicits her favorite feelings.

Jim Tigerman, creative director of Tigerdale Studios in Los Angeles, is in the business of fabricating fantasy. He knows the worth of bringing it home. "All too often," says Tigerman, "when people get involved in spending large sums of money on interiors, they get real serious——all the fabrics may be right, say, they all match—but the finished product tends to lack humanity and humor." He has solved the problem with whimsical soft sculptures. Fat ballerina legs are on their toes by his bed. The four blue-toe-shoed legs support a table top. Such humor and playfulness suggest that there is no need to cage ourselves with conventionality.

Respect for your dreams can lead you out of the cage of conventionality

Marjorie Helsel believes that all you need is an attitude of irreverence. Who knows more about you than you? Who else should tell you what to do? You may want to smooth your rough edges so you can fit together with others and have a sense of belonging, but why not celebrate your individuality as well? Total homogeneity becomes boring. Celebrating yourself, extending your sense of fun, not only delights yourself—but others. It allows others to relax and enjoy themselves too. Celebrating your soul is a high. Isn't it high time?

ANTIQUES ARE ALWAYS CURRENT

Why not be surrounded by your favorite things? They bring back happy memories, make you feel good. They also convey your good feelings to others, give a positive impression of you. Showing personal collections is both a source of satisfaction and a source of self-expression.

Andrew Tauber, a young designer notable for his sophistication (and his wonderful whacko sense of humor), collects Louis XVI gilt bronze and Chinese Ch'ien (1736–1795) and K'ang Hsi (1662–1722) furniture, paintings, and porcelain. "Antiques, like anything beautiful, are always current," says Tauber.

Tauber has a secret for evolving excellence in his collection

Loving to buy exquisite objects, but living in a limited space can present a problem. Tauber has devised an ingenious answer. "I think collecting antiques becomes, well, like a disease for many people. They fill up the house, then they add even more. I solved that problem by following one of the first rules of collecting." Tauber's rule is: "I sell three or four pieces and use the money to buy one incredible piece. Friends are always saying: 'You buy more and more each year, but you seem to have less and less.' Now, that's collecting."

How does Tauber fit his furnishings into his rather ordinary apartment?

The rent may be high, but that doesn't mean the apartment is distinguished. It is an ordinary rectangle in a highrise on Manhattan's Upper East Side. The one-room apartment does have a pretty parquet floor and a wall of windows; otherwise there's nothing special about it. With his fine furnishings, how could Tauber adapt to this environment?

"One of the reasons I took (this apartment) is because it is a perfect rectangle. As far as I'm

concerned, this is a neutral space. Neutral space is flexible. Now, if I had a room with all sorts of funny angles in it, I would have to put such-and-such a cabinet in a particular spot. This way, everything (except the screen) has been in a different place at some time." To enjoy his furnishings, Tauber moves them around; he likes to look at them from different angles from different places.

As pictured, his one-room apartment is zoned into three areas. The sleeping function is centered, accommodated by a French campaign bed. His lucite desk and working area are at one end. His sitting and entertaining area is at the other. Areas are defined by small 19th-century rugs. To harmonize with his traditional furnishings, Tauber wanted some sense of softness in the background. He hung drap-

eries with tassles at the windows. However, he didn't want to deny the actual character of the place. He left the brushed steel window fittings untouched. "Some friends urged me to camouflage them with paint," he recalls, "but I didn't think that was appropriate for this apartment."

How did Tauber design the apartment to set off his fine furnishings?

So as not to crowd his furnishings, he keeps them to the minimum, and he strives to make the 27 x 15-foot (8 x 4.6-meter) space seem spacious. Tauber mirrored one wall to expand the space and to reflect the light from the adjacent wall of windows. He kept the area rugs small, so one would still see a space-stretching expanse of pale parquet floor. He painted the walls a wonderful green, inspired by the color of his fabulous Chinese screen. Green is a cool color that recedes from the eye, making the walls appear more distant than they actually are. A bedcovering, similar in color to the walls, also recedes in space. It blends gently into the background.

A modern touch dramatizes the antiques

A most modern lucite table sets a stunning style contrast with Tauber's antiques. Designer Tauber knows that you can emphasize something by contrasting it with its opposite. This see-through background is the perfect foil for his Ch'ien Lung and K'ang Hsi vases and companion for his stunning Ch'ien Lung screen. "That's why I bought the desk," Tauber explains. "I think you have to do one shot of something modern in this setting."

Sources

Lucite desk: ABACUS PLASTICS. Mirrored wall: ADMIRAL GLASS. Fabric on French campaign bed: BRUNSCHWIG & FILS and SCALA-MANDRE.

WHAT ARE YOUR FAVORITE FURNISHINGS?

She is a busy executive who runs at a fast pace. When she comes home, she wants to tune out. No more rushing to meetings. No more jangling phones. No more putting on the pressure to meet deadlines. No more shoes. Home is haven—a place to rest and relax.

How is it possible to create such a space in a rather ordinary apartment in the middle of a busy city? Designers Joseph Minicucci and Jerome Hanauer found a way.

They made the most of their client's collections

Knowing full well that it is comforting to be surrounded by the things you love, the designers ascertained their client's favorite furnishings. A beautiful room-size Kerman rug that had belonged to her mother and a cherished collection of blue and white Chinese porcelain became the stars of the scheme. The designers sought to set off these assets.

The Kerman rug became the focal point of the living room seating area. So as not to compete with the glorious colors of the rug, the modular seating was covered in a neutral color. The coffee table was chosen in see-through glass.

At the entry, the porcelain collection creates an exciting event. To complement the collection, the designers covered the walls in blue lacquer. Then they set up the dishes against a dramatic backdrop of white. This modular storage system houses the eye-catching objects at a variety of levels. Furthering the effect, track lighting on the ceiling is directed to spot the stars. An Oriental runner on the floor gives completion to the blue design theme—as well as a connection to the living room beyond.

Enhancing the sense of entry, and furthering the effect of their client's collection, the designers chose antique carved ebony screens with blue and white porcelain inserts to flank the walls at the end of the entry. The screens create a sense of division between the entry and the living room and give more archi-

tectural interest to the ordinary apartment. There was a practical purpose too. Something structural was needed at the point where the blue walls ended and the white walls began; otherwise the effect would seem arbitrary, not architectural.

Another set of screens flank the windows in the dining room. This brings the blue and white porcelain theme deep into the space, harmonizing the whole. Notice also that pieces of porcelain are grouped on the coffee table, on an end table, and on an antique altar facing the seating. Porcelain pieces enchant the eye all around. This even, attractive distribution of accessories gives unity to the design and gives the client the sense of being surrounded by the things she loves.

The designers made the most of the view

The highrise apartment did have an asset of its own: a view of the backyard gardens of the adjacent townhouses. Luckily, the apartment was at a level where it was possible to really see the trees and enjoy them. The designers brought the arbor indoors with plenty of plants and trees. They covered the windows with skinny-slat blinds to control the light without diminishing the view. What could be more relaxing than a trip to the country (within a city space)?

Emphasized furnishings are traditional; others are simple, modern

Recognizing that their client was a traditionalist at heart, but a practical person as well, designers Hanauer and Minicucci produced an effective eclectic mix. Simple, modular, or massive shapes set off the detail and intricate interest of traditional forms. The one emphasizes the other. A modern travertine table shows off the beguiling curves of Queen Anne chairs. The simple modular seating forms a frame for the ravishing rug. The total effect creates a haven to satisfy the soul.

Sources

Storage wall system: SCHOOL-FIELD FURNITURE INDUSTRIES. Ceiling track light: LIGHTOLIER. Antique ebony screens with porcelain inserts: HENDRICK IMPORTS. Dining table of filled travertine: RAYMOR. Dining chairs: HICKORY FURNITURE COMPANY. Chandelier: LOUIS MATTIA. Seating units and ottomans: KAYLYN (subsidiary of HICKORY FURNITURE CO.). Upholstery fabric, tussah silk: FAR EASTERN FABRICS. Travertine end tables and pedestal: RAYMOR. Cocktail table: SELIG. Antique altar table: HENDRICK IMPORTS. Bronze (nickel-plated) sculpture: FRANZ HAGENAUER, 1929. Plants: KING EXOTIC.

THE MAGIC OF CARPETS

The young couple wanted to escape the city in the summers. They found a house in Elberon, New Jersey.

The designer brought in the colors of sun, sand, and sky

New York designer Samuel Botero knew the New Yorkers' need for a sense of space and sunshine. White walls and nothing but simple shades at the windows let in light and reflect it around the room. The pleasures of bare feet on the beach are suggested by wall-to-wall sand-colored sisal matting. A sand-colored seating chaise, centered in the living room, blends into the open ambience. Sky-blue floor pillows provide additional inexpensive seating.

To emphasize openness, storage is built in

While repositioning the stairway, Botero accommodated the couple's need for storage space by building in closets on either side of the new stairs and recessed a living room bar into the place of the previous stairs.

To cover up an ugly radiator in the dining area, Botero built a Formica shelf the whole length of the wall and underneath put a removable wood grille. It both hides the radiator and conceals storage space.

The carpets make the magic

To make their summer house a home and to give a comforting continuity to their lives, the couple rolled up their favorite possessions and brought them with them. Their fine collection of flat-woven kilim carpets give flair and a personal air to the summer house.

Sources

Sisal matting: PATTERSON, FLYNN & MARTIN. Pale blue denim for pillows: KIRK-BRUMMEL. Paintings on mantel by BOB and JUDY NATKINS. Oriental rugs: THE PILLOWRY. Radiator cover: top by FORMICA, wooden grille by VENT WOOD. Recessed lights in bar, Luxo lamp: HARRY GITLIN.

129

Photography by Richard Champion

THE HUMAN TOUCH OF HANDCRAFTS

As an antidote to mass-produced anonymity, handcrafted objects bespeak personality. They are one of a kind, and they express loving labor. Somebody cared enough to take the time. Somebody dared enough to give expression to his/her creative urge. The naive simplicity of some handcrafts makes us realize that life need not be so complicated. We can live in a simple, symbiotic harmony with nature.

Handcrafts suggest a sense of living, breathing life

Gere Kavanaugh enhances her sense of living by surrounding herself with handcrafts. Katchina dolls by Steve Schuck hang over her living room mantle. A painting by Jules Engles is suspended from the ceiling, as is a handmade advent wreath candelabra. Gere Kavanaugh designed the top of the coffee table herself. She created a flowerlike design with tiles. To cover the seat of a mass-produced Breuer chair, Kavanaugh stitched a flower design in needlepoint. The commonplace chair becomes something uniquely personal.

With handcrafted painted designs, Kavanaugh brings the abundance of nature indoors

Inspired by the vitality of the painted houses she saw on a trip through Bavaria, Gere Kavanaugh determined to bring the beauty of the southern California landscape into her own Westwood home. She covered her window with a trellis and painted growing grapes around the frame. She colored the arched entrance to the living room sunny sky blue. She made an arbor of an arched passageway by painting leaves up, over, and around. She painted a curved telephone nook like the inside of an apple barrel, piled high with fresh-picked fruit. The abundance of nature is all about. For her bedroom, Kavanaugh designed a fabric sprinkled with

flowers. She uses the design both for a bedspread and for draperies around the bed, so she indeed sleeps in a garden of delights.

There is no austerity in Kavanaugh's concept of "back to nature." There is joy. And there is a joy she can share. An award-winning designer of furniture and fabrics, Gere Kavanaugh also designs commercial and residential interiors and exhibition spaces. To all this work, she brings the humanizing touch of handcrafts to hearten the spirit and to give individuality to each interior.

Sources

Sheepskin rug in living room: THE TANNERY. Flower table: top designed by Kavanaugh; base by JERRY ROTHMAN; tile by STONELIGHT TILE CO. Bedroom fabric, designed by Kavanaugh, printed on American cotton by her firm, GERALDINE FABRICS.

LIVING FANTASIES

THE PARTY'S NEVER OVER!

Designer Marjorie Borradaile Helsel, ASID, likes to entertain. Six chairs in leather and six in Larsen's butterflies are spread throughout her Manhattan apartment to allow for large or small dinner parties. "I see nothing disturbing in covering a Louis XVI chair in Larsen's contemporary butterflies or piercing African carvings for kitchen cabinet pulls. A certain fantasy emerges with the unexpected, which delights the adult eye as cartoons do the child's." Helsel's ability to excite the eye, and the imagination, with welcome surprises makes her a delightful hostess, as well as a delightful designer.

And Helsel knows how to entertain herself. "I believe fantasy is as important in our private rooms as it is in public ones. All it takes is a little irreverence!"

Helsel has a wrap-around mural of her friends partying in her bedroom

She commissioned artist S-H. A. Booker to paint a mural in her bedroom. It took three years to complete. "We worked out the concept together. It was to have a party mood filled with friends, someone serving champagne, a Mary Petty-type maid bringing in wondrous flowers, . . ." she remembers. "It was no accident that the characters took on the likenesses of my friends. What could be better than having your friends around you?"

The friends not only make Helsel feel good; they make the room look better. The scale of the figures, she believes, makes the room appear larger than it actually is. To coordinate, furnishings were underplayed with an aubergine cotton—which matches the "dinner clothes" of the guests.

Helsel has created her own private world where her wishes come true. The party's never over!

Sources

Louis XVI armchairs: upholstered in apricot leather from AMERICAN LEATHER. Louis XVI side chairs: upholstered in printed velvet from JACK LENOR LARSEN. Dining table on a gilt metal base with a faux marble top, painted to look like antigua verde. Painting to the right of louver door: MANUEL PRIOR.

S-H. A. Booker's mural extends around the room. The lady languishing on the chaise recalls the real recamier below. Reproduction Louis XVI chaise: WYCOMBE-MEYER. Italian Louis XVI side chairs upholstered in Thai silk from JACK LENOR LARSEN. Carpet: STARK. Chandelier: NICCOLINI. Antique French consulate table: GILBERT PELHAM.

Photography by Ken Howard

CREATURE COMFORTS

Photography by David Glomb

Jim Tigerman is the Creative Director of Tigerdale Studios in Los Angeles. "L.A. is ninety percent fantasy," Tigerman states. "It's not tied down to conventional design. It reflects a more casual attitude, a less structured set-up." If L.A. is a land of fantasy, Tigerman is one of its creators. Designing displays for movie sets, TV studios, stores, and other interiors, Tigerman knows how to arrest the eye and free the imagination from its conventional cage. His own home had to satisfy his spirit, his eclectic eye, his simultaneous desires for comfort and excitement. He designed it himself.

Tigerman's home is full of fantasy and humor

"All too often," says Tigerman, "when people get involved in spending large sums of money on interiors, they get real serious—all the fabrics may be right, say, they all match—but the finished product tends to lack humanity and humor." Tigerman doesn't believe in following any set design discipline. He serves his own humanity by surrounding himself with the things he loves. "I enjoy many different types of atmospheres and objects," he confides, "from Chinese silk weaving to Sheffield silver to stuffed elephants." (He has Oriental scrolls *and* a stuffed elephant in his bedroom.) His favorite objects make him feel at home, and they inspire his creative eye. "Different types of forms and different types of materials constantly keep you going visually," explains the Creative Director.

Soft sculpture has become a favorite for him

"I started working in plaster and moved into bronze and glass-blowing," Tigerman recalls. But then he found fabric to be more flexible and fun. A "very *direct*" medium—he calls it—no waiting for the metal to heat or the glass to cool. "Soft sculpture puts humanity and humor back into an environment," he allows. "A piece can be functional, but it also adds something special to an environment."

His bedside table is a case in *pointe*. Four chunky ballerina legs in blue toe shoes support the table top. Despite their girth, the legs provide a light touch. In back of the bed, by the window,

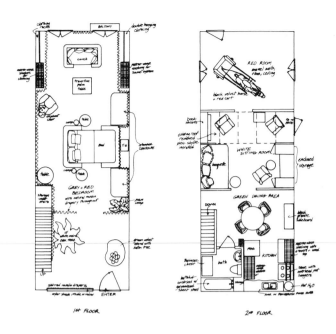

1st FLOOR   2nd FLOOR

one can see an elephant trunk raised in the air. This is a chair in gray wool and mohair, designed by Tigerman's assistant Gail Anne Gibson and intended as a giveaway on a TV game show. A plaintive pet, a stuffed rabbit, waits for attention at the end of the bed. Upstairs, in a fire-engine-red room, a black-fabric carousel horse pulls a red-satin-trimmed cart by silk reins. When not used as a stable, the red room doubles as a dining room. ("It's one of the most wonderful colors to have a dinner party in—people sit there and *glow*.") Tigerman likes the horse, though; he feels it's useful "to lighten up the atmosphere." One gets the irrepressible feeling that here any childhood (or adult) fantasy *could* come true! Tigerman's home is an illustration that he can make pipe dreams come true with more than pipe cleaners.

A fabricator of fantasies, Ti-gerdale Studios markets a line of soft sculptures, including six sorts of trees, various cacti, animals, and rocking pigs, bears, and kangaroos for children. The Studios do custom design too. As a special present for Mr. Stigwood of the Robert Stigwood Organization, they worked with the company's emblem, linking it with some Japanese symbol for fertility and creating a 7-foot (2.7-meter) loveseat of a stuffed red cow.

Tigerman expresses himself with more than sculpture

His bedroom was dark. Light only entered at one end. What could he do to lighten and brighten the atmosphere? He got yards and yards of 120-inch (3-meter) unbleached natural muslin sheeting. "We just went wild with a staple gun," he confesses, "and covered the whole room." The curtains cover shelving, clothing, and the TV. For now-you-see-it, now-you-don't changes, Tigerman rigged up tie-backs and finished them off with ceiling "rosettes" he created out of scalloped shapes of the material. The TV, amusingly, is at center stage at the back of his bed.

His bed is proportioned like an enormous, protective play-pen. A loveseat by the windows echoes its shape in smaller scale.

Upstairs in the green dining area adjacent to the kitchen, the lacquered dining chairs look chic and sleek. But they too are provocatively playful. The arms flow into elephant heads. The legs, naturally enough, are elephant trunks.

Between the green dining room and the red occasional dining room (stable) is a transitional sitting space with white walls and a partial skylight. The bathroom is a shiny space, lined with galvanized metal sheeting. Here, in this home, one gets to experience oneself in all sorts of ways. There is no conventionality to dull the senses with monotony. There is the zestful liberation of play. This home is both Tigerman's creative expression and his inspiration.

Sources

Miles of muslin: CANVAS SPE-CIALTY CO., L.A. Black chamois pony and cart, designed by GAIL ANNE GIBSON OF TIGERDALE STU-DIOS.

GROOVIN' IN A TOMB

Do you dare have your wildest dreams come true? Seems that Hollywood producer Allen Carr does. Wanting to enhance his reputation as an innovator of excitement and wanting to impress his jaded "I-have-seen-everything" Hollywood cohorts, he was up for doing the dramatic.

Carr wanted to build an Egyptian tomb as a disco in his own home

Nobody had done that before. This would be the very first Egyptian-tomb disco ever built in a private home. Bizarre idea. A silent repository for the dead becomes an encasement for loud jungle heart-beat rhythms, flashing lights, and gyrating bodies. Kinky, maybe. Kicky, certainly.

How could Carr turn his fantasy into reality? Carr went to Phyllis Morris, a flamboyant designer in the L.A. area. She liked the idea of groovin' in a tomb. With her design director, Stephen Reiman, she worked out a somewhat authentic tomb with all sorts of opulent, outrageous—downright decadent—aspects.

The tomb is entered through a bronze verde-gres door, embellished with an Egyptian symbol of life. Copper and gold palm trees are by the bar. Deeper in the space is the disco. Walls are covered with copper-colored mirror. The copper metal dance floor has inset lighting which flashes in rhythm with the music. (It is computer-programmed to respond to the vibrations in the air.) Lounging banquettes by the dance floor are covered in a metallic material—handwoven copper. Shiny satin pillows pick up reflections of the flashing lights. A ceiling of bronzed, inverted pyramids of infinity lighting further stimulates the senses. The sensuality of the space is completely unrestrained—and unforgettable.

If, as King Tut thought, real life is in the afterworld, Allen Carr and his friends are sure practicing for a good time. If all there is is now, then Allen Carr shows us that the outrageous isn't impossible.

Photography by Sheldon Lettich

INDEX OF DESIGNERS/ARCHITECTS

The following is a list of the designers whose work is shown in this book. As is clear from the content of the book, designers *do* make it their business to satisfy the practical and emotional needs of their clients. They know how to translate vague yearnings into colors, textures, styles—all the ingredients that together combine to make your own personal place.

If you would like to take advantage of a designer's expertise to clarify your own thinking about your home, I recommend it as a shortcut to self-expression. You might hire a designer for a simple consultation, to get a clearer focus on your ideas. Alternately, you can hire a designer to execute the entire job—do all the planning, purchasing, and supervision of outside contractors. This does not mean that you opt out of the creative process. You still must express your needs and desires. It's the designer's challenge to fulfill them. After all, it's *your*

home, not his or hers.

If you're wondering where and how to find a designer you might like, may I recommend calling the local chapter of the American Society of Interior Designers (ASID). So as not to show preference, the chapter will give you three or four names of designers to interview.

You also might find a designer in the design department of a retail store you trust. In-store designers might be members of ASID or of IDS (the Interior Design Society).

When interviewing, you might ask about a designer's education and experience in order to establish his or her expertise, but more important, trust your own intuition. Is this a person with whom you feel at home? With a designer, you have to "be at home" in order to make a home.

DIRECTORY OF DESIGNER SOURCES AND SHOWROOMS

You have probably noticed that "Sources" are provided at the end of each project in this book. The fine manufacturers, importers, and craftsmen listed allow the designer to implement his/her artistry. Without such sources, designers would be left with nothing but ideas and naked rooms.

The listing of sources in this directory includes those referred to in the text that are likely to serve you and your designer. (Most sources are exclusively "to the trade" so that you can get in only when accompanied by your designer. Before you get mad at being excluded, consider that "to-the-trade" showrooms save manufacturers from checking a zillion credit references and allow them to afford floor space for special items that wouldn't appeal to a mass market.)

The sources here tend to have wide marketing distribution. By contacting the company at its headquarters listed below, you can find out where its products are available in your area. Many regional or esoteric sources are not included in this directory to save you (and us) the frustration of not being able to find them conveniently.

Abacus Plastics Inc.
102 W. 29 St., New York, NY 10001
212/947-8990

Abraham-Zumsteg, Inc.
979 Third Ave., New York, NY 10022
212/355-4010

Abstracta Structures, Inc.
38 W. 39 St., New York, NY 10018
212/944-2244

Acoma
415 N.E. 62 St., Miami, FL 33138
305/751-2202

Admiral Glass Co.
440 Third Ave., New York, NY 10016
212/532-9787

Airborne/Airconas Corporation
580 Orwell St., Mississauga, Ontario L5A 3V7 Canada
416/272-0727

Ain Plastics Inc.
300 Park Ave. S., New York, NY 10010
212/473-2100

Altman, B., & Co.
Fifth Ave. & 34 St., New York, NY 10016
212/689-7000

Amana Refrigeration Inc.
Amana, IA 52204
319/622-5511

American Drapery & Carpet Co., Inc.
257 Park Ave. S., New York, NY 10010
212/477-9400

American Leather Mfg. Co.
2195 Elizabeth Ave., Rahway, NJ 07065
201/382-1700

American Olean Tile Co.
1000 Cannon Ave., Lansdale, PA 19446
215/855-1111

American-Standard
P.O. Box 2003, New Brunswick, NJ 08903
201/885-1900

Apollo Woodworking & Metal Corp.
3482 Park Ave., Bronx, NY 10456
212/993-7247

Architectural Supplements, Inc.
341 E. 62 St., New York, NY 10021
212/758-5406

Ardee Floor Coverings, Inc.
129 W. 30 St., New York, NY 10001
212/868-4080

Astrup Co., The
2937 W. 25 St., Cleveland, OH 44113
216/696-2800

Atelier International, Ltd.
235 Express St., Plainview, NY 11803
516/935-6700

Azuma
666 Lexington Ave., New York, NY 10022
212/752-0599

B & B America
745 Fifth Ave., New York, NY 10022
212/752-5234

Bac Street Antiques
8428 Melrose Pl., Los Angeles, CA 90069
213/653-3899

Baker Knapp & Tubbs, Inc.
917 Mdse. Mart, Chicago, IL 60654
312/329-9410

Barrett, David, Inc.
131 E. 71 St., New York, NY 10021
212/472-8521

Benjamin Moore & Co.
51 Chestnut Ridge Rd., Montvale, NJ 07645
201/573-9600

Beshar, A., & Co., Inc.
49 E. 53 St., New York, NY 10022
212/PL8-1400

Bloomingdale's
1000 Third Ave., New York, NY 10022
212/355-5900

Boccia, Thomas J., designer
137 E. 57 St., New York, NY 10022
212/688-4034

Boyd Lighting Co.
56 12 St., San Francisco, CA 94103
415/431-4300

Braun Construction Co.
P.O. Box 22727, Savannah, GA 31403
912/232-6482

Brickel Associates, Inc./Ward Bennett Designs
515 Madison Ave., New York, NY 10022
212/688-2233

Brown Jordan Co.
P.O. Box 5688, El Monte, CA 91734
213/443-8971

Brown, Paul, Inc.
306 Stuart St., Boston, MA 02116
617/542-0131

Brunschwig & Fils
410 E. 62 St., New York, NY 10021
212/838-7878

Burge, Yale R., Reproductions Inc.
315 E. 62 St., New York, NY 10021
212/TE8-4005

Burke, Charles, Lighting
8912 Ashcroft Ave., Los Angeles, CA 90048
213/550-1100

Burlington Industries Inc.
1345 Ave. of Americas, New York, NY 10019
212/333-5000

Business Equipment Inc.
2 Park Ave., New York, NY 10016
212/481-0800

California Glass
8605 Kewen Ave., Sun Valley, CA 91352
213/875-0060

Canvas Specialty Co., L.A.
7344 Bandini Blvd., Los Angeles, CA 90040
213/722-1156

Carpets From Longon Inc.
919 Third Ave., New York, NY 10022
212/838-4783

Casa Bella Imports, Inc.
3750 Biscayne Blvd., Miami, FL 33137
305/573-0800

Castelli Furniture Inc.
950 Third Ave., New York, NY 10022
212/751-2050

Cenci Inc.
306 Stuart St., Boston, MA 02116
617/542-0131

Center Bros. Inc.
P.O. Box 22278, Savannah, GA 31403
912/232-6491

Chambers Corp.
P.O. Box 927, Oxford, MS 38655
800/647-5162

Champion International Corp., Building Products Div.
One Champion Plaza, Stamford, CT 06921
203/358-7000

China Seas Inc.
979 Third Ave., New York, NY 10022
212/752-5555

Clarence House
40 E. 57 St., New York, NY 10022
212/752-2890

Classic Galley Inc.
2009 Fulton Place, High Point, NC 27263
919/886-4191

Cody, E.G., Inc.
80 N.E. 40 St., Miami, FL 33137
305/374-4777

Connaissance Fabrics Inc.
979 Third Ave., New York, NY
10022
212/679-8899

Conrad Imports
714 Sansome St., San Francisco,
CA 94111
415/434-2789

Corian Building Prods.
E.I. DuPont De Nemours & Co.,
Inc.
Wilmington, DE 19898
302/774-8471

Corning Glass Works
Houghton Park, Corning, NY
14831
607/974-9000

Corvin Chairs, Inc.
503 E. 72 St., New York, NY
10021
212/BU8-6380

Country Floors, Inc.
300 E. 61 St., New York, NY
10021
212/758-7414

Couristan, Inc.
The Carpet Ctr., 919 Third Ave.,
New York, NY 10022
212/371-4200

Creative Woodworking Co., Inc.
1370 Ralph Ave., Brooklyn, NY
11236
212/451-0460

De Angelis, Perry, Woodwork
15 W. 20 St., New York, NY
10011
212/929-6520

Decorative Tiles Inc.
10 N.E. 40 St., Miami, FL 33137
305/576-7844

Del Piso Tile Co.
1637 S. State College Blvd.,
Anaheim, CA 92806
714/634-4776

Dennis And Leen Inc.
612 N. Robertson Blvd.,
Los Angeles, CA 90069
213/652-0855

De Saavedra, Rubén
225 E. 57 St., New York, NY
10022
212/759-2892

Design International, Inc.
3544 North Miami Ave.,
Miami, FL 33127
305/576-0616

Descon Woodworking Company
100 Spring St., Ossining, NY
10562
914/941-5383

Design South
10214 N.W. 80 Ave.,
Hialeah Gardens, FL 33016
305/557-0782

Didonato, Richard T., contractor
2039 Blackrock Ave., Bronx, NY
10472
212/823-7756

Donghia Furniture Co., Ltd.
315 E. 62 St., New York, NY
10021
212/935-4707

Draperies for Home & Industry
Inc.
156 Fifth Ave., New York, NY
10010
212/242-2804

Edison Price Inc.
409 E. 60 St., New York, NY
10022
212/838-5212

Edlin, Jules, Inc.
330 E. 59 St., New York, NY
10022
212/753-4220

Elkay Manufacturing Co.
(Stainless Steel Sinks)
2222 Camden Court, Oak Brook,
IL 60521
312/986-8484

Elon Inc.
150 E. 58 St., New York, NY
10022
212/759-6996

Endurance Floor Co. Inc.
14200 N.W. 7th Ave., Miami, FL
33168
305/681-4923

Esquire Carpet Corp.
136 E. 57 St., New York, NY
10022
212/421-8880

Far Eastern Fabrics Ltd.
171 Madison Ave., New York,
NY 10016
212/MU3-2623

Foro Marble Co. Inc.
18 Whitwell Pl., Brooklyn, NY
11215
212/852-2322

Fields, Edward, Inc.
232 E. 59 St., New York, NY
10022
212/759-2200

Fine Arts Furniture Inc.
351 E. 61 St., New York, NY
10021
212/759-1414

First Editions Wallcoverings &
Fabrics, Inc.
979 Third Ave., New York, NY
10022
212/355-1150

Flexco, Div. of Textile Rubber
Co., Inc.
E. Sixth St., Tuscumbia, AL
35674
205/383-7474

Foam-Tex Co., Inc.
51 E. 21 St., New York, NY
10010
212/674-8440

Formica Corp.
Berdan Ave., Wayne, NJ 07470
201/831-2000

Forms & Surfaces
P.O. Box 5215, Santa Barbara,
CA 93108
805/969-4767

Fortuny Inc.
509 Madison Ave., New York,
NY 10022
212/PL3-7153

Fotia Stone Inc.
54-41 59 St., Maspeth, NY 11378
212/894-4555

Four Seasons Import Inc.
220 Fifth Ave., New York, NY
10001
212/684-2050

Galerie 99
1135 Kane Conc.,
Bay Harbor Island,
Miami, FL 33154
305/865-5823

Gatewood, William
2247 Cove Ave., Los Angeles,
CA 90039
213/689-9180

General Electric Co.
570 Lexington Ave., New York,
NY 10022
212/750-2000

Geraldine Fabrics
1792 Kelton, Los Angeles, CA
90024
213/826-5215

Ghiordian Knot, Ltd., The
1050 Second Ave., New York,
NY 10022
212/722-1235

Gitlin, Harry, Inc.
305 E. 60 St., New York, NY
10022
212/751-7130

Gratale, Carole, Inc.
979 Third Ave., New York, NY
10022
212/838-8670

Gretchen Bellinger Inc.
979 Third Ave., New York, NY
10022
212/688-2850

Groundworks, Inc.
231 E. 58 St., New York, NY
10022
212/620-0700

Habitat Inc.
341 E. 62 St., New York, NY
10021
212/758-5406

Hall, Frank A., & Sons Ltd.
969 Third Ave., New York, NY
10022
212/HA1-3140

Halo Lighting, Div. McGraw-
Edison Co.
400 Busse Rd., Elk Grove, IL
60007
312/956-8400

Harmer Rooke Gallery Ltd.
3 E. 57 St., New York, NY 10022
212/751-1900

Harmony Carpet Corp.
979 Third Ave., New York, NY
10022
212/355-6000

Harris, S., & Co., Inc.
580 S. Douglas St., El Segundo,
CA 90245
213/973-7402

Hastings Tile & Il Bagno
Collection
410 Lakeville Rd., Lake Success,
NY 11042
516/328-8600

Heina, William J., & Son
1556 Third Ave., New York, NY
10028
212/369-8500

Helikon Furniture Co., Inc.
607 Norwich Ave., Taftville, CT
06380
203/886-2301

Heller Designs Inc.
41 Madison Ave., New York,
NY 10010
212/685-4200

Hendrick Imports Ltd.
50 E. 13 St., New York, NY
10003
212/673-9863

Henri Bendel Inc.
10 W. 57 St., New York, NY
10019
212/247-1100

Hess, Richard
Southover Farm, Roxbury, CT
06783
203/354-2921

Hexter, S. M., Co.
2800 Superior Ave., Cleveland,
OH 44114
216/696-0146

Hickory Furniture Company
P.O. Box 998, Hickory, NC
28601
704/322-8624

Hillside Glass Co. Inc.
197039 Jamaica Ave., Hillside,
NY 10469
212/464-7200

Hinson & Co.
251 Park Ave. S., New York, NY
10010
212/475-4100

Holland Shade Co., Inc.
306 E. 61 St., New York, NY
10021
212/644-1700

ICF Inc. (Intl. Contract Frnshs.)
145 E. 57 St., New York, NY
10022
212/752-5870

Interface Flooring Systems
Orchard Hill Rd., LaGrange,
GA 30241
404/882-1891

Interior Designers Inc.
380 N.E. 60 St., Miami, FL 33137
305/754-1646

Intrex Inc.
341 E. 62 St., New York, NY
10021
212/758-5406

Janus Et Cie
8687 Melrose Ave., Space 146,
Los Angeles, CA 90069
213/652-7090

Jones, Paul M., Inc.
979 Third Ave., New York, NY
10022
212/753-0288

Kagan, Vladimir, Designs Inc.
232 E. 59 St., New York, NY
10022
212/371-1512

Katzen, Lila
345 W. Broadway, New York,
NY 10013
212/431-9439

Kay, Frank, Ltd.
232 E. 59 St., New York, NY
10022
212/PL8-0917

King Exotic Plants
774 Ave. of Americas,
New York, NY 10001
212/684-8396

Kirk-Brummel Associates
979 Third Ave., New York, NY
10022
212/477-8590

Kneedler-Fauchere
8687 Melrose Ave., Los Angeles,
CA 90069
213/855-1313

Knoll International
The Knoll Bldg.,
655 Madison Ave.,
New York, NY 10021
212/826-2400

Koch & Lowy, Inc.
21-24 39 Ave., Long Island City,
NY 11101
212/786-3520

Kohler Co.
Kohler, WI 53044
414/457-4441

Kovacs, George, Lighting, Inc.
230 Fifth Ave., New York, NY
10001
212/683-5744

Lahey, George
126 Madison Ave., New York,
NY 10016
212/684-6767

Larsen, Jack Lenor, Inc.
41 E. 11 St., New York, NY
10003
212/674-3993

Lazarus, M.H., & Co., Inc.
516 W. 34 St., New York, NY
10001
212/LO3-5250

Lee/Jofa
351 Park Ave. S., New York, NY
10010
212/889-3900

Len-Mar Industries, Inc.
401 N.W. 71 St. (West Bldg.),
Miami, FL 33150
305/751-3779

Les Prismatiques
Fine Arts Bldg., 232 E. 59 St.,
New York, NY 10022
212/832-8107

Levolor Lorentzen, Inc.
1280 Wall St. W., Lyndhurst, NJ
07071
201/460-8400

Light/Inc.
1162 Second Ave., New York,
NY 10021
212/838-1130

Lighting Associates, Inc.
305 E. 63 St., New York, NY
10021
212/751-0575

Lighting By Kenneth, Inc.
3816 N.E. First Ave., Miami, FL
33137
305/573-5040

Lightolier Inc.
346 Claremont Ave., Jersey City,
NJ 07305
201/333-5120

London-Marquis Inc.
639 N. La Peer Dr., Los Angeles,
CA 90069
213/274-3312

**Los Angeles, County Of, Art
Museum**
5905 Wilshire Bldg.,
Los Angeles, CA 90025
213/937-4250

Louis Mattia
980 Second Ave., New York, NY
10022
212/753-2176

Louverdrape, Inc.
1100 Colorado Ave.,
Santa Monica, CA 90401
213/450-6100

Love, Diane, Inc.
851 Madison Ave., New York,
NY 10021
212/879-6997

Luxo Lamp Corp.
Monument Park, Port Chester,
NY 10573
914/937-4433

M.W.G. Inc.
3630 N.E. First Court, Miami,
FL 33137
305/576-8111

Macy's
Manhattan Herald Square,
New York, NY 10001
212/971-6000

**Magee Carpet Co., Div. Shaw
Ind., Inc.**
P.O. Box 2128, Dalton, GA
30720
404/278-3812

Mann, Karl, Associates
232 E. 59 St., New York, NY
10022
212/MU8-7141

Manno Upholstering Inc.
12 E. 12 St., New York, NY
10003
212/929-0120

Mariano Studios
255-04 Northern Blvd.,
Little Neck, NY 11362
212/428-2524

Martin/Brattrud, Inc.
22500 S. Vermont Ave.,
Torrance, CA 90502
213/775-6751

**Mascheroni, John, Signature
Collection Ltd.**
979 Third Ave., New York, NY
10022
212/753-9166

McGuire Company, The
38 Hotaling Place, Jackson Sq.,
San Francisco, CA 94111
415/986-0812

Mid-State Tile Company
Cohon Grove Rd., Box 1777,
Lexington, NC 27292
704/249-3931

Miller, Herman, Inc.
8500 Byron Rd., Zeeland, MI
49464
616/772-3300

Milliken, Alexander F., Gallery
98 Prince St., New York, NY
10012
212/966-7800

Mittman, Louis, Co., Inc.
214 E. 52 St., New York, NY
10022
212/888-5580

Mittman, M., & Co. Inc.
307 E. 53 St., New York, NY
10022
212/PL3-6390

Mitsu Novelties Inc.
25 W. 35 St., New York, NY
10001
212/947-7892

Morris, Robert
12 Greene St., New York, NY
10013
966-5154

Niccolini
57 E. 11 St., New York, NY
10003
212/254-2900

Nita Designs Ltd.
173 North Central Ave.,
Valley Stream, NY 11580
516/872-8988

Objects Plus Inc.
1164A Second Ave., New York,
NY 10021
212/832-3386

Ochs, Rhoda, Gallery
595 Middle Neck Road,
Great Neck, NY 11023
516/487-9891

Oscar Cabinet Shop
9368 N.W. 13 St., Miami, FL
33139
305/592-5066

Pace Collection Inc., The
11-11 34 Ave., Long Island City,
NY 11106
212/721-8201

Palacek Imports L.A.
1933 S. Broadway, Los Angeles,
CA 90007
213/748-9563

Panner Woodworking Co., Inc.
40 W. 24 St., New York, NY
10010
212/675-2045

Patterson, Flynn & Martin, Inc.
950 Third Ave.
New York, NY 10022
212/751-6414

Paul Associates, Inc.
155 E. 55 St., New York, NY
10022
212/755-1313

Payne Fabrics
3500 Kettering Blvd., Dayton,
OH 45401
800/543-4322

Peerless Rug Ltd.
P.O. Box 944, Place
Bonaventure, Montreal
H5A 1E8 Quebec, Canada
514/866-5821

Pengelly, Charles, Collections
119 N.E. 39 St., Miami, FL 33137
305/573-2339

Phoenix Carpet Co. Inc.
979 Third Ave., New York, NY
10022
212/758-5070

Pillowry, The
177 E. 87 St., New York, NY
10028
212/369-1300

Pivot Design Services, Inc.
1 W. 72 St., New York, NY 10023
212/799-7150

Plant Specialists, Inc.
524 W. 34 St., New York, NY
10001
212/279-1500

Pratt & Lambert Inc.
75 Tonawanda St., Buffalo, NY
14207
716/873-6000

Presto Glass Co.
561 W. 181 St., New York, NY
10033
212/795-0822

Raymor/Moreddi Inc.
734 Grand Ave., Ridgefield, NJ
07657
201/941-0220

**Rennert Manufacturing
Company, Inc.**
93 Greene St., New York, NY
10012
212/925-1463

Ronald Charles Associates, Inc.
3900 N. Miami Ave., Miami, FL
33137
305/573-3900

Roper Corporation
1905 West Court St., Box 867,
Kankakee, IL 60901
815/937-6000

Rosecore Carpet Co. Inc.
979 Third Ave., New York, NY
10022
212/421-7272

Roseline Products Inc.
120 Schmitt Blvd., Farmingdale,
NY 11735
516/293-8234

Saporiti Italia
225 E. 57 St., New York, NY
10022
212/371-3700

Savnik & Co.
601 McClary Ave., Oakland, CA
94621
415/568-4628

Scalamandre
950 Third Ave., New York, NY
10022
212/361-8500

Scandinavian Design Inc.
127 E. 59 St., New York, NY
10022
212/755-6078

Schlussel, Alan
201 E. 71 St., New York, NY
10021
212/535-3509

Schoolfield Furniture Industries
200 Lexington Ave., New York,
NY 10016
212/686-3074

Scott, Isabel, Fabrics Corp.
245 Newtown Rd., Plainview,
NY 11803
516/249-3100

Sears, Roebuck and Co.
1 Sears Tower, Chicago, IL
60684
312/875-2500

Showroom III
30 Hotaling Place, San
Francisco, CA 94111
415/421-8922

Smith & Watson
The Decorative Arts Ctr.
305 E. 63 St., New York, NY
10021
212/355-5615

**Sonneman-Kayson Lighting
Corp.**
37-50 57 St., Woodside, NY
11377
212/651-8000

Sormani Mfg.—Linea Plus Ltd.
964 Third Ave., New York, NY
10022
212/753-0956

Stark Carpet Corp.
979 Third Ave., New York, NY
10022
212/PL2-9000

Stendig Inc.
410 E. 62 St., New York, NY
10021
212/838-6050

Stiffler, Ed, Flowers
1190 Third Ave., New York, NY
10021
212/628-4404

Stonelight Tile Co.
1651 Pomona Ave., San Jose, CA
95110
408/292-7424

Stratton Industries, Inc.
P.O. Box 1007, Cartersville, GA
30120
404/382-9350

Stroheim & Romann
155 E. 56 St., New York, NY
10022
212/691-0700

Sunar
730 Fifth Ave., New York, NY
10019
212/246-5200

SVP Kitchens & Bath Designs
505 Park Ave., New York, NY
10022
212/752-4596

Tannery, The
2801 Leavenworth,
San Francisco, CA 94133
415/885-2990

Thermador
6135 District Blvd., Los Angeles,
CA 10040
213/562-1133

Thonet Industries
491 E. Princess St., York, PA
17405
717/845-6666

Thorp
245 Newton Rd., Plainview, NY
11803
516/249-3100

Tigerdale Studios Inc.
1931 Bay, Los Angeles, CA
90021
213/489-4255

**Tradewinds Outdoor Furniture
Corp.**
16301 N.W. 15 Ave., Miami, FL
33169
305/624-4411

**Tressard Fabrics &
Wallcoverings, Inc.**
979 Third Ave., New York, NY
10022
212/752-3510

Tuscan Wood Art Corp.
1228 Second Ave., New York,
NY 10021
212/861-6671

Unitex Industries Inc.
1375 Merchandise Mart,
Chicago, IL 60654
312/467-1267

Vanleigh Contract Corp.
4900 Hampden Lane, Bethesda,
MD 20014
301/657-3900

Vogue Enterprises Inc.
21 E. 40 St., New York, NY
10016
212/685-4268

V'Soske Shops, Inc.
155 E. 56 St., New York, NY
10022
212/688-1150

Wagner, Sherle, International
60 E. 57 St., New York, NY
10022
212/758-3300

Waldo's Designs
620 North Almont Dr.,
Los Angeles, CA 90069
213/659-6757

Wall Trends, Inc.
17 Milweed Way, Avenel, NJ
07001
201/382-8600

**Wascon & Burns Construction
Co.**
32-30 58 St., Woodside, NY
11377
212/278-2000

**Weaver's Domain/Window
Modes**
979 Third Ave., New York, NY
10022
212/355-7763

**Westchester Custom Kitchens
Inc.**
145 East Post Rd., White Plains,
NY 10601
914/946-8100

Wiremold Corporation
Woodlawn St.
West Hartford, CT 06110
203/233-6251

Wolf-Gordon Wallcoverings
132 W. 21 St., New York, NY
10011
212/255-3300

**Wood-Craft Cabinet &
Hardware Co.**
1106 E. 59 St., Savannah, GA
31404
912/355-7920

Woodson Wallpapers
200 Lexington Ave., New York,
NY 10016
212/684-0330

Workbench, The
470 Park Ave. S., New York, NY
10016
212/532-7900

Workman, Alene S.
Creative Environs of Lynn
Wilson Associates, Inc.
4041 La Guna Ave., Coral
Gables, FL 33146
305/442-4041

Wycomb-Meyer Co.
305 E. 63 St., New York, NY
10021
212/753-2010

Zimmerman, C. & J., Corp.
919 Third Ave., New York, NY
10022
212/486-9212

Zographos Design Ltd.
150 E. 58 St., New York, NY
10022
212/421-6650